Cambridge Elements

Elements in the Psychology of Religion
edited by
Jonathan Lewis-Jong
St Mary's University Twickenham and University of Oxford

RELIGION AND FOOD

Alexandra S. Wormley
University of Michigan

Adam B. Cohen
Arizona State University

Shaftesbury Road, Cambridge CB2 8EA, United Kingdom

One Liberty Plaza, 20th Floor, New York, NY 10006, USA

477 Williamstown Road, Port Melbourne, VIC 3207, Australia

314–321, 3rd Floor, Plot 3, Splendor Forum, Jasola District Centre, New Delhi – 110025, India

103 Penang Road, #05–06/07, Visioncrest Commercial, Singapore 238467

Cambridge University Press is part of Cambridge University Press & Assessment, a department of the University of Cambridge.

We share the University's mission to contribute to society through the pursuit of education, learning and research at the highest international levels of excellence.

www.cambridge.org
Information on this title: www.cambridge.org/9781009671446

DOI: 10.1017/9781009421898

© Alexandra S. Wormley and Adam B. Cohen 2025

This publication is in copyright. Subject to statutory exception and to the provisions of relevant collective licensing agreements, no reproduction of any part may take place without the written permission of Cambridge University Press & Assessment.

When citing this work, please include a reference to the DOI 10.1017/9781009421898

First published 2025

A catalogue record for this publication is available from the British Library

ISBN 978-1-009-67144-6 Hardback
ISBN 978-1-009-42187-4 Paperback
ISSN 2753-6866 (online)
ISSN 2753-6858 (print)

Cambridge University Press & Assessment has no responsibility for the persistence or accuracy of URLs for external or third-party internet websites referred to in this publication and does not guarantee that any content on such websites is, or will remain, accurate or appropriate.

For EU product safety concerns, contact us at Calle de José Abascal, 56, 1°, 28003 Madrid, Spain, or email eugpsr@cambridge.org

Religion and Food

Elements in the Psychology of Religion

DOI: 10.1017/9781009421898
First published online: November 2025

Alexandra S. Wormley
University of Michigan

Adam B. Cohen
Arizona State University

Author for correspondence: Alexandra S. Wormley, awormley@umich.edu

Abstract: Religion plays an important role in what and how we eat. Indeed, food is a critical component of religion – as well as a reflection of the other components that make religion unique. This fact is what necessitates greater attention toward food as a lens for understanding psychological phenomenon both within the psychology of religion and the social scientific community at large. Utilizing theories and exemplars from multiple disciplines, the authors discuss how food relates to four dimensions of religion – beliefs (Section 2), values (Section 3), practices (Section 4), and community (Section 5). Throughout the Element and in a concluding section, the authors provide exciting directions for future research. In addition to providing a review of our current understanding of the role of food and religion, this work ultimately seeks to inspire researchers and students to investigate the role of food in religious life.

Keywords: food, religion, culture, religious community, religious practices

© Alexandra S. Wormley and Adam B. Cohen 2025

ISBNs: 9781009671446 (HB), 9781009421874 (PB), 9781009421898 (OC)
ISSNs: 2753-6866 (online), 2753-6858 (print)

Contents

1 Introduction   1

2 Beliefs   3

3 Values   12

4 Practices   22

5 Community   31

6 Conclusion   37

References   43

1 Introduction

In an era of globalization, it is hard to name a meal more well-known around the world than the Big Mac. McDonald's iconic burger features two hamburger patties, a slice of American cheese, lettuce, pickles, onions, and the eponymous "Big Mac Sauce." The United States sold over 560 million Big Macs in 2007 alone, or 1.86 burgers for every one American (ABC News, 2009). While practically synonymous with McDonald's, the Big Mac is not present in all of the 40,000 stores operating internationally. What could drive this megacorporation to abandon its iconic sandwich?

Religion. Approximately one in every three McDonald's in Israel adheres to *kosher* principles, which forbid the combination of meat and dairy products. In North India, the Big Mac – and any beef or pork products – are missing entirely from the menu, replaced with chicken and veggie burgers. McDonald's in Pakistan can also assure customers that their Big Macs contain *halal* meat, slaughtered and prepared in line with the Islamic tradition.

Food is a critical part of our daily lives and affects how we think and feel (Cohen et al., 2016; Gómez-Pinilla, 2008; Rozin et al., 2019). For humans, selecting what to eat is not an inherently simple task, given our wide diet and complex social norms (Pollan, 2010; Rozin, 1976). By some estimates, we make over two hundred food-related decisions a day (Wansink & Sobal, 2007) and it is easy to see how. At a standard US McDonald's, consumers must choose between nine different hamburgers – not to mention the accompanying side, drink, and their respective sizes. And these decisions come only after deciding to eat, driving to that McDonald's and debating whether to go through the drive-thru or go inside. All of this, for one meal.

Religion is a powerful guide in the decision of what to eat. For example, many religions possess rules for what (not) to eat, resulting in broad systems like *halal* or *kashrut* for adherents to follow. Religions also provide guidance on how to eat – only after sunset or always before? in a community or alone? with a blessing before, after, or both? However, the relationship is bidirectional; food also plays a role in constituting religious experiences. A description of Ramadan would be incomplete without mentioning fasting. Consumption of the consecrated bread and wine as part of the sacrament of Holy Communion has been a defining (and distinguishing) feature of Christianity since its inception. Hindus and Shintoists leave elaborate spreads of food for gods at temples and shrines.

Our goal in this Element is to discuss religion and food. First, it is important to define what we mean by religion. Defining religion is notoriously difficult; to do so is to take "a wanton risk of intellectual confusion" (Nash, 1913, p. 1;

Streng, 1972). To begin, Merriam-Webster defines religion as "a personal set or institutionalized system of religious attitudes, beliefs, and practices." When people think of religion, they likely call to mind one of these "institutionalized systems" such as Christianity, Hinduism, Islam, Buddhism, or Judaism. Indeed, in this Element, we will also focus on these major world religions as they represent the bulk of extant research on food and religion. However, William James preferred to focus on "personal religion" rather than institutional component, defining religion in his lecture series on the topic as "the feelings, acts, and experiences of individual men in their solitude, so far as they apprehend themselves to stand in relation to whatever they may consider the divine" (James, 1902). But other scholars, such as Durkheim (1915) and ourselves (Cohen, 2009; Wormley et al., 2023), include the institutional component in their definition of religion.

In acknowledgment of the multidimensional nature of religion, the four dimensions of religiosity model proposes that religion can be understood as spanning four dimensions: cognitive, moral, emotional, and social (Saroglou et al., 2020). In other words, religion consists of:

1. beliefs: the doctrinal claims about the nature of reality, especially as they pertain to life, death, and the existence of deities.
2. values: the guiding moral principles of a religious group which motivate thoughts, feelings, and behavior.
3. practices: the ritual behaviors of a religious group.
4. community: the identity, roles, and institutions that bind adherents into a religious in-group.

We use these four dimensions as a framework for guiding our discussion of the role of food in religious life, as it covers much (but certainly not all) of religion.

Further, it is important to recognize that religious life is incredibly diverse, but current scholarship is concentrated on the world's major religions, especially Christianity. This bias is further compounded by the fact the psychology of religion has largely used Western samples so even our findings about well-researched religious groups may be skewed by the broader culture they are embedded in. For example, though we know quite a lot about American Christians, our understanding of, say, Korean Christians and how Korean culture intersects with Christian culture is lacking. Thus, in addition to limited information on smaller religious groups, we will also not be able to fully capture variation in religious life *within* these groups. As a result, we avoid making statements about food and religion writ large and acknowledge that there will always be exceptions to some of the claims we make within this

Element. This diversity in religious life is what makes the study of religion both fascinating and complex.

Despite the important and diverse role of food in religious and secular life, the intersection of religion and food has gone relatively understudied. In a chapter on the matter, Corrie Norman points out that much of the literature on religion and food tends to focus on religious food taboos with scholars being "more fascinated with fasting and forbidden food than with calorie-laden religious foodways" (Norman, 2012, p. 410). However, the role of food in religion is far more complex. As Kaori O'Connor (2008, p. 152) writes, researchers "have long recognized that food is not just feed ... Both symbol and substance, food embodies history, memory, tradition, invention, place, diaspora and cultural values, and reflects both continuity and change."

The goal of this Element is to provide an overview of the relationship between religion and food – beyond the study of "fasting and forbidden food" – and to capture how food embodies religion and its history. Ultimately, we hope to show that any description of religion would be remiss without exploring how it intersects with a critical part of life: eating. In each section, we discuss how food relates to the four dimensions of religion – beliefs (Section 2), values (Section 3), practices (Section 4), and community (Section 5). Within each section, we provide a brief description of that dimension then connect it to illustrative examples from fields such as psychology, religious studies, anthropology, and sociology. Throughout, we connect examples back to theories, such as cultural evolution and social identity theory. In the spirit of inspiring more research within this domain, we conclude each section and the Element as a whole with open questions for research (Section 6).

2 Beliefs

On November 11, 1215, the Fourth Lateran Council convened at the behest of Pope Innocent III. The agenda was full – in the next nineteen days, the Council would compose seventy-one papal decrees. These canonical laws covered topics such as nepotism (Canon 31) and an early description of the separation of church and state (Canons 42 & 44). The final canon would mark the start of the Fifth Crusade as June 1, 1217 (Duggan, 2011). But at the front of everyone's minds was the problem of bread and wine – or was it the body and blood of Jesus?

The debate was over the particulars of a historical dinner. At the Last Supper, Jesus of Nazareth would sit His twelve disciples at a table and foretell of the remainder of His life. That night's meal – unleavened bread (in alignment with the Jewish tradition of Passover) and wine – would be the basis of a ritual of remembrance of Jesus' sacrifice: the Eucharist.[1]

Twelve centuries after this dinner, a new generation of disciples would gather at the Vatican to debate precisely what happened in the moment a priest consecrated the bread and wine. The Book of Matthew records Jesus as saying, "'Take and eat; this is my body... This is my blood of the covenant'" (Matthew 26:26-28). Did this mean that the bread and wine were the literal body and blood of Jesus? If so, what happened to the bread and wine? Was it destroyed? Could the bread coexist alongside the body? The Council would eventually decide that "His body and blood are truly contained in the sacrament of the altar under the forms of bread and wine, the bread and wine having been changed in substance, by God's power, into His body and blood" (Macy, 1994; *The Fourth Lateran Council*, 1215). This declaration meant that "the Body of Christ" would simultaneously refer to three things: the literal body of Jesus Christ, the bread and wine that were consumed, and the community who partake of that body. Not everyone would agree with the Council's decision and this process, known as *transubstantiation*, would be a cornerstone of on-going conflict between traditions of the Christian faith.

Beliefs around Holy Communion presented another conundrum for Protestants in the late nineteenth century during the rising temperance movement. Temperance had been pushed by the American Temperance Society which consisted largely of middle-class evangelicals (Rohrer, 1990). However, each Sunday, they were expected to partake in a small amount of alcohol. How could they reconcile their social beliefs about alcohol with their religious faith? The answer would be grape juice – a convenient and similar-enough alternative to wine. An entrepreneur would capitalize on this change, giving rise to a fruit juice empire – Welch's. More recently, in 2003, the Vatican clarified that while gluten-free bread is insufficient for the practice, those with celiac disease may participate with only wine (Congregation for the Doctrine of the Faith, 2003). The ongoing conundrum of communion is just one example of how critically important food can be in understanding religious beliefs, the subject of this section.

Food lies at the center of many religious beliefs, the cognitive components of religion. Beliefs encapsulate what it means to be alive, what it means to be human, the purpose of one's existence, and how that existence came to be. These beliefs form the basis of religious life, guiding the values, practices, and communities we will discuss later, and shape the secular world as well. The seemingly mundane – unleavened bread, figs, butter – can take on entirely new meaning when embedded within one's religious beliefs. In this section, we

---

[1] *Eucharist* refers to both the ritual and the consecrated bread and wine, while Holy Communion refers to the action of receiving that Eucharist.

outline where food takes the spotlight in three themes of religious beliefs: stories about the world, social hierarchies, and the afterlife.

2.1 The Psychology of Beliefs

In an early treatise, William James (1889) described beliefs as "the mental state or function of cognising reality." Today, we define religious beliefs as the guiding frameworks of a religion which outline answers to questions, especially existential questions (Saroglou, 2011). Many religious traditions provide answers to these, among other, questions:

1. How did humans come to exist?
2. Who should be in charge?
3. What happens after death?

With these answers, individuals develop a subjective truth about how the world works. Answers may be derived from religious texts, oral traditions, and one's own synthesis. Religious beliefs may also be shaped by other cultural identities (Settles & Buchanan, 2014; Wormley et al., accepted in principle). For example, there are regional differences in the practice of Christianity, which reflect the blending of the religious tradition with local culture. This is especially apparent in the practice of Christianity within Africa, where imported Christian traditions were blended with traditional beliefs and practices extant in the region ("syncretism"). This has led to a proliferation of a unique form of Christianity that blends Pentecostal beliefs with traditional forms of worship and indigenous healing practices (Amenga-Etego et al., 2021; Fernandez, 1978; Meyer, 2004; Mofokeng, 2024; Pew Research Center, 2006). Even within the same church, cultural identities may clash. During fieldwork in one Chinese Catholic church in Boston, a scholar noted parishioners from Hong Kong and Fujian had largely isolated themselves from one another, adopting different practices within the parish (e.g., using their English vs. Chinese names; Xiong, 2023).

Beliefs form a fundamental basis from which individuals act upon the world. Thus, to properly understand an individual's psychology, you must understand their belief system. A simple analogy can be drawn from political beliefs – an American's decision to vote for a conservative political candidate makes sense if you know this person believes in limited governance, restrictions on abortion, and opposes affirmative action. In the same way, religious beliefs predict prosocial behavior (Johnson et al., 2016), coping strategies (Pargament et al., 1998), and self-control (Rounding et al., 2012), among other psychological outcomes.

In addition to helping us understand the individual, religious beliefs are critical to understanding differences between groups (Cohen, 2009). Beliefs surrounding communion represent a key difference between Protestantism and Catholicism – two religious traditions which are remarkably similar in their belief system. However, doctrine dictates that Catholics should believe in transubstantiation – the bread and wine *literally become* the body and blood of Christ. Yet, Protestants are generally taught to deny transubstantiation, even if they believe that Christ is somehow present in the Eucharist. As these two groups diverged on the basis of their beliefs, they developed different traditions and communities which further served to differentiate between the two groups and, in some cases, led to conflict.

Similar processes can be seen in other religious traditions. The *Sunni* and *Shia* traditions of Islam differ in their beliefs about how leadership should be passed on within the faith, how the faith will be revived by the *Mahdi*, and which *hadiths* should be followed. Reform and Orthodox Judaism differ in their beliefs about who wrote the *Torah*, how the *Torah* should be interpreted, how the *Torah* should be applied to life, and how Jewish practices should (or should not) be integrated with modern secular culture. The Catholic Church and Eastern Orthodox Church famously split in 1054 along geographic lines – partially due to theological differences surrounding the use of leavened or unleavened bread during communion. Thus, diverging beliefs – including those regarding food – certainly play a core role in differentiating and dividing religions and individuals.

2.2 Myths

A critical component to many religions is holy texts: the *Qur'an,* the Bible, the Book of Mormon, the Epic of Gilgamesh, the *Guru Granth Sahib*, for example. These books outline the core beliefs of a faith and, often, the events that led to the creation of mankind, deities, and the religion. Being a part of daily life, food often appears in these texts as they describe what adherents should do, what early figures in the faith ate, or as easily accessible metaphors for describing complex spiritual phenomena (e.g., in Hinduism the universe was creating by churning an ocean of milk; Mahias, 1987). The significance of food within a religion may be derived from their role in these texts. For example, of Jesus' dozens of recorded miracles in the New Testament, five had to do with providing food for others in times of need. The book of Matthew describes the miracle of the "Feeding of the Five Thousand":

> And when it was evening, his disciples came to him, saying, This is a desert place, and the time is now past; send the multitude away, that they may go into

the villages, and buy themselves victuals. But Jesus said unto them, They need not depart; give ye them to eat. And they say unto him, We have here but five loaves, and two fishes. He said, Bring them hither to me. And he commanded the multitude to sit down on the grass, and took the five loaves, and the two fishes, and looking up to heaven, he blessed, and brake, and gave the loaves to his disciples, and the disciples to the multitude. And they did all eat, and were filled: and they took up of the fragments that remained twelve baskets full. And they that had eaten were about five thousand men, beside women and children.

- Matthew 14:15-21, King James Version

Another example of the importance of food in foundational stories lies within Islam. Dates are mentioned in the *Qur'an* twenty-two times. According to a *hadith*, the Prophet used them to break fasts which some followers of Islam continue to do during Ramadan. Lending itself toward a functional explanation for the purpose of food prescriptions, the Prophet Mohammad also explicitly described how dates possess health benefits, especially during pregnancy and labor (Surah Maryam 19:23). Thus, the significance of dates within the Islamic tradition is derived from beliefs about their *Qur'anic* significance.

Food is also critically important in the Hebrew Bible. In the garden of Eden, Adam and Eve are expelled because they ate fruit from the tree of the knowledge of good and evil, which had been forbidden to them (Genesis 2). Later in the book of Genesis, God grudgingly allows the Jewish people to eat meat, after the flood, but with some stipulations (e.g., blood cannot be consumed, for it is the life of the animal; a limb cannot be torn from a living animal; Genesis 9). These two examples, among many more food rules and stories in the Hebrew Bible, are already telling about a Jewish worldview – that vegetarianism is the moral ideal, and that animals must be treated with compassion and respect, even as they are slaughtered for food (Brook, 2009). Each of these biblical injunctions gave rise, over the course of cultural evolution, to very complex sets of rules comprising the *kashrut* system (Cohen, 2021).

While food rules vary across even Abrahamic traditions (Muslims and Jews are prohibited from eating pork, but not Christians), there is one food that unites these Abrahamic traditions: *manna*. *Manna* is referred to as a supernatural substance sent from Heaven to feed the Israelites. It is unclear what manna actually was; some hypothesize that it was the sugary secretion of certain insects (Donkin, 2013), while others argue that it was beads of lichen (Haupt, 1922). *Manna* is a holy food – central to beliefs about the role of God in rescuing the Israelites from starvation in the Abrahamic religions. Yet, it is unique in the fact that it does not play a role in modern Abrahamic rituals due to the ambiguity about what *precisely* it was.

Certainly, the role of food in religion is not uniquely Abrahamic. Within Greek myths specifically, the significance of food was often spelled out in in stories about deities. Pantheons feature major and minor deities which may specialize in a particular food stuff as the "God[dess] of Some Food." For example, Dionysus was considered the Greek god of wine. His parallel was Osiris within the Egyptian mythology and Bacchus in Rome. From this, we get stories about the debauchery following drunken bacchanals inspired by the god of wine. These stories teach us when and why we might consume wine, as well as the consequences of its consumption.

Religious stories about food are often used to explain the realities of the local ecology. The Greeks also explained the change of the seasons and harvesting patterns through the story of Hades, Persephone, and her mother, Demeter. Each fall, Hades would steal Persephone from her mother. In her grief, Demeter would make the world cold. When Persephone would return each spring, she would bring good weather for the start of the next agricultural cycle. Thus, the Greek mythos provides structure for understanding the climatic factors that impact the availability of food. In the Blackfoot tribe, the prairie turnip is a critical source of protein and starch. The plant is said to have heavenly origins, being brought to the people by the daughter-in-law of the Moon (Kehoe, 2002; LaPier, 2018; Trombley, n.d.). Here too, we see an example of indigenous religions explaining the state of their agriculture via stories of creation.

From these examples, we can conclude that the significance of food within religious traditions often originates from their role in holy texts and stories. These stories are a vehicle for social learning of religious beliefs, values, and practices (Oman, 2013). More broadly, Cohen has theorized that religious texts and histories exert causal influences on the formation of later religious cultures, shaping things like moral judgments and what it means to be a person (Cohen, 2009, 2015). So too it seems for food practices. In modern practices, the persistence of food is a symbolic (and occasionally functional) means of worship and remembrance. To break one's fast with dates during *Ramadan* is to engage in a historic and richly symbolic practice. To take communion within a Catholic Church is a demonstration of worship and delineation from other religious traditions. To break unleavened bread on Passover is to participate in a centuries-old tradition in remembrance of liberation from bondage. To invite others to join in the Passover seder ("let all who are hungry come and eat") is to relive and share a pivotal historical event with others and apply the meanings to today's world. Yet, what ties these practices together is their basis in complex religious beliefs about the origin and persistence of the world.

2.3 Hierarchies

Religious beliefs often touch on social status. Social Dominance Theory suggests that societies from group-based hierarchies, upheld by "legitimizing myths." Religion can provide such myths to define and justify this inequality (Sidanius & Pratto, 1999). Perhaps the most famous example of this within religion is the traditional caste system in India which is shaped in part by one's religious affiliation. The simplest description of this caste system places religious leaders at the top of these hierarchical systems and menial laborers at the bottom (Dumont, 1980).

Because social hierarchy often mirrors economic means, there are both *de facto* and *de jure* restrictions on food consumption by one's position in the hierarchy. Within the social hierarchy, there may be rules about what members can eat (Smith, 1990). Brahmans, at the top of India's caste system, should only eat the finest food, or *pakka* (as opposed to *kacca*, inferior food). These rules may be enforced through economic practicalities; ghee (clarified butter) is necessary to make *pakka* but is expensive, preventing those from lower castes from accessing it (Sharma, 2021). When consumed, these foods cue others as to one's social status and reinforce one's own place in the social hierarchy.

Certain food items may also be reserved for the highest social status – that of a god (Beerden, 2012). Ambrosia and nectar were the foods of the gods in Greek mythology as they conferred immortality. Occasionally, a mortal Greek hero would be given ambrosia or nectar. After being killed, Patroclus' body is embalmed with ambrosia and nectar to preserve it forever (Zanni, 2008). Sarpedon – who was killed by Patroclus – was also anointed with ambrosia in the Iliad (Haupt, 1922). Food may also take on inedible forms for the divine. In the Zinacanteco Mayan religious tradition, food for the gods is the result of burning items: white candles are tortillas and tallow candles are beef (Stross, 2010; Vogt, 1976). Additionally, venerated figures might confer preference for a particular food. While the Prophet Mohammad favored dates, Krishna is known to like butter. Thus, dates are traditionally used to break Islamic fasts in imitation of Mohammad and *ghee* became a critical food within Hinduism.

Preferred foods may be associated with particular characteristics of deities which may serve as a mechanism to reinforce beliefs. While most of deities in the Lucumí tradition tend to "have a sweet tooth," different *orishas* having different preferences: "The elderly, imperturbable creator spirit *Obatalá* eats meringues and rice puddings prepared with white sugar – all relatively soft foods that may be gummed by those without teeth… Fiery masquerader *Oyá* devours *torrejas*, the 'Spanish French toast' that dresses up day-old bread in egg, milk, and cinnamon sugar" (Pérez, 2014, pp. 181–182). As research from cognitive psychology suggests, pairing specific foods with *orisha* characteristics may help practitioners internalize their personalities and mythos through sensory memory (Shams & Seitz, 2008).

Lastly, while food itself may symbolize one's status, the preparation and consumption of food also conveys social status. Preparation of religious foods tends to confer higher status onto individuals. The fact that food can only be certified as adhering to the complex rules of *kashrut* by a trained *mashgiach* in Judaism, confers status onto that individual. Similarly, within Roman Catholic mass, the consecration of the bread and wine for Holy Communion can only be done by an ordained Catholic priest; authority over significant rites such as this provides additional status in that social group. Food consumption also confers cues to the social status of individuals. For example, ritual alcohol consumption in the Mayan religious tradition "emphasizes social continuity, serving all from same shot glass; but, at the same time, hierarchical discontinuity of age and sex through the order of serving..." (Stross, 2010; Vogt, 1976, p. 41). In sum, beliefs around social hierarchy within a religious group are reflected in what is consumed, how it is prepared, and how it is consumed.

2.4 Afterlife

Religions often provide adherents with an explanation for what happens after death. What awaits us on the other side? Are we gone forever? Are we reincarnated? Can we reconnect with our life on Earth? Beliefs surrounding death and the afterlife may feature foodstuffs as a metaphor or a means for connecting this world and the next. Here, we explore two traditional practices that do not necessarily belong to a particular religious affiliation but certainly represent spiritual and existential beliefs; cultural traditions such as these underscore the blurry line between culture, spirituality, and religion.

Though their physical body may be gone, some spiritual traditions state that the dead must still eat. Among Chinese in the city of Fuzhou, sending ancestors to the grave with food, as well as regular sacrificial offerings, is a way to ensure health for the living and the dead. *Qi*, a cosmic force between the physical and metaphysical, connects ancestors and descendants to one another, even beyond the grave. One such sacrificial food is *aojiu*, a rice porridge originating from a Chinese folk story of a son trying to feed his hungry mother in the afterlife. Such sacrificial foods ensure that the souls of the ancestors can be nourished; as Emily Wu notes "since the well-being of the ancestors affects the well-being of the living descendants, once the ancestors are in a better state of being (and when they can be sustained with regular worship), the descendants also benefit from the healing process" (Wu, 2018, p. 28). Beyond this indirect effect, living descendants benefit from the *aojiu* directly; food from offerings is typically consumed shortly after offerings at the shrine. And far from being a sweet treat, *aojiu* contains healthful foods such as seeds and nuts known for their medicinal benefits in Chinese medicine.

Similarly, *Dia de los Muertos* (Day of the Dead) is a traditional Mexican holiday when living descendants bring the favorite foods of the deceased to their grave. The living also indulge in holiday-specific food: *pan de muerto* and sugar skulls (Rushing, 2008). Though unaffiliated with a specific religious tradition *per se*, the spiritual undertones of *Dia de los Muertos* are strong; these practices imply the existence of an afterlife wherein loved ones can reconnect with the dead and share a meal.

Reminders of the afterlife have a range of psychological effects. The theory of terror management suggests that when faced with one's own mortality, religious individuals reaffirm their beliefs in a higher power as a way to protect their worldview (Vail et al., 2009, 2012). At the national level, countries that believe more in hell – but not heaven – show lower rates of crime, which scholars suggest is due to concerns about the eternal consequences of one's wrongdoing (Shariff & Rhemtulla, 2012). From these two findings, we can see that reminders of the afterlife shape human cognition and behavior. When engaging in these rituals involving food and the afterlife, we might expect concrete downstream consequences, such as increased religiosity.

2.5 Open Questions

Clearly, beliefs around food embed these foodstuffs with important symbolic meaning. However, it remains unclear whether practitioners actively consider the symbolic component when consuming these foods. For example, does the average Muslim breaking fast with dates do so to intentionally engage with a belief about the significance of dates? Or do they do so out of routine? When taking communion, does the average Catholic dwell on the question that plagued the Fourth Lateran Council: is this truly the body of Christ? Survey work from Pew Research Center suggests that seven in ten Catholics in the United States do *not* believe that the bread and wine are the body and blood of Christ (Smith, 2019). Additional work is needed to investigate what goes on in the minds of practitioners when they consume religiously significant food and whether these beliefs predict greater religiosity or community engagement.

Further, given the wide array of the human diet (Pollan, 2010), why these particular foods? Why does the ritual of communion utilize bread and wine? Why does *Dia de los Muertos* offer sweet foods and not savory ones? A cultural evolution approach may offer some hypotheses. Cultures and religions may be more inclined to promote healthful foods if they are meant to be a part of everyday diet. This can be seen in the Mormon church's prohibition on tobacco and alcohol. In excess, both can be dangerous; thus, to build a healthy congregation, a religion is incentivized to place prohibitions on unhealthy food items, which can be explained through broader beliefs and value systems. In contrast, to demarcate special or holy days, religions may encourage the consumption of difficult-to-make dishes or unique flavors.

2.6 Conclusion

Food plays a central role in our religious beliefs: how we came to be, how we stack up in societies, how we will move into the next life. As we will see in later sections, the centrality of food in religious beliefs can be understood through the centrality of food in daily life – what is a better miracle for the starving than providing food? What better way to connect with the deceased than through a meal just like when they were living? However, questions remain about how actively we consider the sacredness of the foods central to our belief system and how we might leverage existing religious belief systems to address societal problems and health concerns. Further, the study of food may contribute to our understanding of existing theories, such as Social Dominance Theory and cultural evolution, by providing a space for demonstrating how, for example, food contributes to upholding and demarcating social elites.

3 Values

Worldwide, over four million individuals identify as Jains and adhere to the principle of *ahiṃsā*, or "not harming" (Evans, 2014; Sen, 2007). To achieve this, Jains are vegetarians to prevent the slaughter of animals, including avoiding eggs. Additionally, Jains may also avoid eating root vegetables to avoid killing any organisms that might be killed as vegetables are pulled from the ground. Stale food should be thrown out in case microorganisms have grown on it. Fruits with many seeds should be avoided because seeds represent a potential life form. They must also only eat while the sun is out to ensure that they can see that their food is truly free of any life forms (Sangave, 1980; Sen, 2007).

What does one gain from following the protocols of the Jain diet? For Jains, this practice ensures more than just preventing violence to other life forms. The definition of violence within Jainism extends beyond harm done to others to include the harm inevitably done to oneself by harming others. Ultimately, the goal of living a nonviolent life guided by the principle of *ahiṃsā* is to escape a cycle of reincarnation.

This Jain worldview is a wonderful example of how food and moral worldviews are mutually reinforcing. In this section, we discuss how within religious contexts, food practices often come to embody certain moral values: cleanliness, charity, mindfulness, nonviolence. These values are embedded in what we eat and how we eat it. Eating certain foods may promote certain values within oneself and one's community. The practices surrounding its consumption may also reflect values – mindful eating promotes quiet contemplation and oneness with the world; avoiding unhealthy foods reflects the importance of religious values surrounding healthy eating and self-respect; ritual food preparations and blessings can be representation of "cleanliness is next to godliness" or thankfulness for the food itself. After all, "you are what you eat."

3.1 The Psychology of Values

Values describe what matters to us and our social groups (Sagiv & Schwartz, 2022). Schwartz outlines six basic principles of values:

1) Values are beliefs linked to affect.
2) Values represent desired goals.
3) Values are relatively stable across situations.
4) Values dictate what the standard is.
5) Values are organized into a hierarchy by priority.
6) Values' placement in this hierarchy guide actions (Schwartz, 2012).

Importantly, one's values shape one's actions (Roccas, 2005; Schwartz, 2012), as values dictate what actions are "good" and "bad." One's moral values also play an important role in self-identity (Aquino & Reed II, 2002; Boegershausen et al., 2015). Therefore, we should be able to infer values from one's actions within some degree of fidelity (Bardi & Schwartz, 2003); an individual that values tradition should embrace traditional ideas and customs; an individual who values hedonism should seek out gratifying experiences. Indeed, as with belief systems, values predict psychological outcomes such as well-being (Sagiv & Schwartz, 2000), political orientation (Jost et al., 2003), and goal pursuit (Kasser & Ryan, 1996). Because eating and other food-related behaviors occur in the real world, food is an ideal vector for understanding the underlying values of an individual and their broader social group, as individuals should consume food in ways that align with their values (e.g., buying organic foods if you value the environment; Grunert & Juhl, 1995).

What foods can and cannot be eaten can provide much broader clues about the worldviews of people from those religions, as famously and brilliantly explicated by Mary Douglas in *Purity and Danger* (Douglas, 1978). With a focus on the Old Testament, Douglas outlines how food rules are complex and unlikely to have any single coherent explanation. Still the rules surrounding food reflect a view of order; often, prohibited foods are ones that are out of place – for example, birds that cannot fly (e.g., ostriches) or sea animals that do not swim (e.g., crabs). Broadly, this reflects and instills a greater belief about order and social hierarchy.

While theories have identified some universal values, cultures and religions will vary in where these values are placed in relative importance to one another (Hofstede, 2001; Inglehart & Baker, 2000; Roccas, 2005; Schwartz, 1992, 2007). For example, Protestant nations score higher on measures of self-expression relative to Catholic nations (Inglehart & Baker, 2000). Broadly, religious individuals tend to value traditionalism and conformity but not self-direction (Saroglou et al., 2004). In addition, we should observe some variation *within* religious groups on the relative importance of values, as they interact with other social identities (e.g., tradition is likely more important to an older Protestant than a younger one, as the importance of tradition varies across the lifetime; Datler et al., 2013). Further, the values which are emphasized vary over the course of a year. Norman provides this example from Islam: "The Muslim values of piety, honor, hospitality, and charity are emphasized in varying combinations on different holiday occasions. For example, honor and hospitality are emphasized in marriage feasts while piety and charity feature in Ramadan fast-breaking meals" (Norman, 2012, p. 417).

A key process underlying the relationship between religious values and foods is rules of "sympathetic magic," as it is classically called in anthropology, including the law of "contagion" (Frazer, 1951). As described by early anthropologists and psychologists, contagion is a principle that suggests that when two things come into contact (e.g., a person and a food), these two things permanently exchange "essences" (e.g., purity or masculinity). This prevalent thought pattern is embodied in the adage "you are what you eat" (Nemeroff & Rozin, 1989; Rozin et al., 1992, 1996). For example, pregnant women in Cameroon avoid eating meat from wild animals lest their children behave like wild animals as well (Asi et al., 2018). Similarly, the ancient Greeks suggest that eating the nightingale would cause insomnia (Rozin, 2014). Further, in many Asian religions, eating pungent vegetables and spices such as garlic are avoided because they "ignite" other passions (Park et al., 2020; Sen, 2007).

Nemeroff and Rozin (1989) further demonstrate this phenomenon in modern Americans. After reading a vignette about "turtle-eaters" and "boar-eaters" undergraduates were more likely to highly rate males in these cultures on traits associated with the species; the turtle-eaters were good swimmers whereas the boar-eaters were more aggressive (Nemeroff & Rozin, 1989). In another study, vegetarians were perceived as being more "plant-like" than "animal-like" (Rozin, 2014). In sum, a consumer is more or less likely to consume an item that does or does not possess the essences or values they seek under the guidance of their religious affiliation.

3.2 Cleanliness

In a sermon from 1778, John Wesley coined the adage "cleanliness is next to godliness." Wesley was not referring to being morally clean, but rather to keeping a clean body and home; the less-often cited preceding line states that "slovenliness is no part of religion." This refrain appears to ring true across many religions; Sikhism, Judaism, Islam, Hinduism, Catholicism, and Buddhism, all prescribe hand hygiene for hygienic and/or ritualistic reasons (World Health Organization, 2009). The idea that religion and cleanliness are linked has also inspired religiously themed hygiene products such as Ivory Soap (named from Psalms 45; Callahan et al., 2010).

It is sensical that our minds find an overlap between physical and spiritual cleanliness. Disgust is an emotion believed to address problems in three different domains: pathogen, sexuality, and morality (Tybur et al., 2009). Imagine your response to finding out someone cheated to get good grades – or seeing a rat in your house. Both situations would likely elicit a disgust response and a desire to avoid such violations of purity. Given the overlap in emotional responses to both moral violations and pathogen threats, it is sensible that religions – more concerned with the former – might adopt rituals designed to alleviate moral and pathogen disgust simultaneously (Terrizzi, 2017).

Food taboos are often justified, among laypeople and academics, through cleanliness arguments. Furthermore, violations of these taboos are punished as moral transgressions. One widely observed food taboo is pork, within Judaism and Islam. One of the textual sources of this taboo, Leviticus 11, directly cites the uncleanliness of the animals unfit for consumption – "Every animal that has a split hoof not completely divided or that does not chew the cud is unclean for you; whoever touches [the carcass of] any of them will be unclean" (Leviticus 11:27; ban reaffirmed in *Al-Qur'an* 5:3). Numerous scholars have speculated about *why* the pig has been deemed unclean. Some have proposed that pork is a vector for trichinosis and its prohibition would reduce the number of cases (Cohen, 2021; Esposito, 2002; Johnson et al., 2015; Terrizzi, 2017); thus, this seemingly arbitrary ban on pork may actually have functional and adaptive significance. However, Wormley and Cohen (2022) demonstrated that pathogen prevalence is not a reliable predictor of the presence of food taboos such as pork; beyond this, the risk of trichinosis is incredibly small and largely avoided by properly cooking pork products. Alternatively, others have suggested that pigs are seen as unclean because they are omnivorous scavengers who will eat carcasses and carrion (Harris, 2012). If we eat something that eats carcasses, we, by extension, eat carcasses – which is moral repugnant on its own (think of eating roadkill directly). Regardless of the functional purpose of the pork taboo, the underlying message is clear: to eat an unclean pig will make you unclean as well. Given that pathogen contamination does not seem to be an apt explanation for meat taboos, perhaps other explanations, such as cultural notions of spiritual purity or costly signaling, should be examined.

In addition to supporting bans on *un*clean foods, religions may have entire diets focused on the consumption of clean foods. Consider the Rastafarian faith and movement. While there is significant diversity in the practice of Rastafarianism, the prescribed *ital* diet emphasizes food that is "pure" because it is all-natural and does not contain processed foods or additives; adherents ascribe to the adage "*ital* is vital." This typically results in a vegetarian diet that also forgoes salt consumption (Powell, 2021). Both examples – the Abrahamic proscription on pork and the pure diet in Rastafarianism – are consistent with the idea of magical contagion. Adherents avoid foods that do not embody their values and conceptions of "purity" lest the impure essence transfer to them. Like Rastafarians, many religious groups adopt the idea of a pure diet; Seventh-day Adventists promote a clean plant-based diet in response to 1 Corinthians 6:19, which states that "your bodies are temples of the Holy Spirit" (a similar sentiment is observed among members of the Church of Jesus Christ of Latter-day Saints; Badanta et al., 2020); the Sattvic diet in the Ayurvedic tradition is also vegetarian, with the added emphasis on easily digestible and nonpotent foods (e.g., onions, garlic); within Islam, *halal* food inherently means safe, good, and pure food.

While some foods may be perceived as "cleaner" than others (often spiritually rather than physically), the value of cleanliness also plays a critical role in the food preparation process. As previously mentioned, religions may prescribe hand hygiene before handling food to avoid pathogens. In Judaism, Talmudic law and tradition dictates that individuals should wash their hands before any meal containing bread; handwashing is featured twice in the traditional *seder* dinner on Passover. For food to be *halal*, adherents are expected to achieve pathogenic purity through proper food handling, preparation, and storage (Abd Rahim et al., 2018).

From an evolutionary perspective, the persistent theme of cleanliness in religion and food is logical. Cleanliness is an adaptive value for religions to promote – healthy adherents create a healthy and sustainable group. Further, there is a clear cognitive and behavioral connection between pathogenic and moral purity based on overlapping evolved responses. But how food has come to embody cleanliness is also unique relative to the other values we will discuss – both the preparation of the food and the food itself plays a role in achieving cleanliness.

3.3 Charity

The idea that one should give back to those in need is ubiquitous across religious groups. For example, Christianity features the parable of the "Good Samaritan" who helps a man in need along the road, despite their ethnic differences; in Indian religions, the practice of *dāna*, or generosity, is ubiquitous. Indeed, some have argued that the idea of being kind to one's neighbor is universal across the world's cultures; it has been dubbed "the Golden Rule" in Christianity, *tzedakah* in Judaism, and *zakat* in Islam but is mentioned in some form in Bahá'í, Buddhism, Confucianism, Hinduism, Greek philosophy, Jainism, Wiccan, and Zoroastrianism.

While a singular food may not embody the value of "charity," food presents an ideal vector for practicing the value of "charity." Per Maslow's hierarchy of needs (Maslow, 1943), spiritual needs are less immediate than basic, physiological needs – such as hunger. Since practical needs present a barrier to achieving spiritual needs, many religious groups focus community aid on tackling basic issues like housing insecurity and hunger for their followers and the broader community. Worldwide, faith-based charities attempt to tackle hunger through programs such as food kitchens, "Meals-on-Wheels," and mutual aid.

Some faith-based food programs are explicitly tied to a religious organization. The Salvation Army provides over fifty million meals to those in need annually and aims to share their Christian faith with those they assist. Members of the Sikh community offer free, regular meals to their community, with no expectation of conversion (proselytization in Sikhism is forbidden). Others are vaguer in their religious affiliations. Take Heifer International, a charity which enables donors to gift livestock to communities in need. For $120, a donor can purchase a goat which "[p]rovides milk, cheese and butter for nourishment, [b]oosts income through sales of extra milk, [and e]ncourages better crop yields by creating fertilizer and clearing land" (Heifer International, 2023). Yet, embedded within this charity is an undertone of religious faith. The organization provides specific fundraising instructions for Christian churches and Jewish *Bar* or *Bat Mitzvah* projects – featuring more prominently on their website than instructions for schools or volunteers to fundraise.

Examples of charity via food abound in religious texts. In biblical law, individuals are obligated to leave the edges of their field for the poor to "glean" food for themselves (e.g., Leviticus 19:9-10). In Hinduism, of all the donations one can provide, *annadāna*, or the giving of food, is declared to be the most important. One section of the *Padma Purana* declares: "Everything is settled in food. Therefore, men particularly desire to give food. There was no gift nor there will be a gift like food."

In sum, most of the world's religions will foster prosocial values of charity and generosity. To better achieve spiritual goals, these religions are incentivized to direct the charitable practices toward meeting basic needs. Through food kitchen and global charities, adherents can act on their value of charity with food as a vector. As one volunteer at a Catholic soup kitchen in California said, "I believe with all my heart that the Lord wants me to do His work, not Mass fifteen times a day" (Clark Moschella, 2002).

3.4 Mindfulness

Korean temple food is a style of food that links traditional Korean cuisine with Buddhist practices. This vegetarian tradition emphasizes natural, healthful foods and the avoidance of pungent vegetables (e.g., onions, garlic), lest the flavors impede spiritual practices. The latter component underscores a key proposition within Korean temple food – food should not impact the spiritual experience.

The consumption of temple food also reflects the Buddhist philosophy of mindfulness: "being attentive to and aware of what is taking place in the present" (Brown & Ryan, 2003, p. 822). As the food is being prepared and consumed, individuals are encouraged to hold positive and flexible thoughts. Adherents report that mindful eating is good for well-being, relaxation, and stress reduction (Park et al., 2020).

Mindfulness may also be induced through the practice of *not* eating. Fasting is relatively common across religious groups but varies in its motivations. For those of the Baha'i faith, a longitudinal study revealed that individuals report greater mindfulness during fasting periods, and that this is positively related to heightened religious experience (Demmrich et al., 2021). However, it remains unclear why fasting invokes mindfulness.

Regardless, mindful eating is becoming increasingly popular both in and out of religious contexts. Practitioners are advised to follow seven steps:

1) Honor the food.
2) Engage all senses.
3) Serve in modest portions.

4) Savor small bites, and chew thoroughly.
5) Eat slowly to avoid overeating.
6) Don't skip meals.
7) Eat a plant-based diet (Hanh & Cheung, 2011).

Mindful eating is also emerging as a promising intervention for promoting healthy eating (Warren et al., 2017); obese individuals who took place in a weekly mindful eating workshop for six weeks saw significant decreases in weight and stress (Dalen et al., 2010). Mindful eating has also been linked to other psychological benefits, including increased overall well-being (Shaw & Cassidy, 2022). Yet, many of these interventions do not invoke religious motivations for mindful eating, despite the fact that the tradition has religious roots (Brown, 2016). Still, religion may be a key mechanism for promoting the success of mindful eating interventions.

3.5 Thankfulness

In the Inuit tradition, seals and hunters have come to an agreement: the seal agrees to be hunted and eaten, so that it might become a part of the Inuit community upon its consumption (Borré, 1991). In return, the Inuit revere the seal for what it contributes to their way of life; disrespecting seals carries ill omens, such as infertility (Peter et al., 2002).

Being thankful for food is a common theme and value across religious traditions. Religious texts and stories abound with descriptions of food as a lifesaving blessing: Jesus feeds the 5,000; the Israelites were saved with *manna*. One should also be thankful for food, even outside of extreme circumstances like starvation. Adherents often express thankfulness during blessings over regular meals. In a Buddhist prayer, speakers "vow to live a life which is worthy to receive [the food]." In the *Qur'an*, readers are told to "Eat of your Lord's provision, and give thanks to Him" (Butash, 2013). Thus, a prominent feature of food practices within religion is to take a moment and be thankful.

Additionally, thankfulness may be formally recognized on religious holidays or auspicious days. In Zoroastrianism, *ajil,* a mix of dried fruits and nuts, is prepared on *gahambars*, seasonal festivals to celebrate thankfulness to God (Mehran, 2019). The Jewish holiday of *Sukkot* is an annual harvest celebration featuring temporary outdoor structures called a *sukkah* (Leviticus 23:42–43) where, traditionally, at least a *kezayit* of bread (approximately the volume of an olive) is eaten on the first night of the week-long celebration (Sukkah 27a). *Sukkot* is a feasting holiday which is meant to celebrate agricultural bounty and gratitude to God for the abundance; some have drawn parallels between it and the American tradition of Thanksgiving (Brumberg-Kraus, 2012).

Religious people tend to exhibit more gratitude and thankfulness – and this gratitude is linked to enhanced well-being (Emmons & Kneezel, 2005; McCullough et al., 2002; Olson et al., 2019; Rosmarin et al., 2011; Tsang et al., 2012). This suggests that gratitude is a key mechanism in the link between religiosity and health. As religions promote thankfulness through values and practice, they may, in turn, be boosting the health of their adherents.

3.6 Nonviolence

As mentioned in the introduction of this section, the pursuit of nonviolence has guided Jains to pursue restrictive diets with strict rituals to ensure that eating does not come at the cost of another life. Principles of nonviolence guide food choices around the world, but perhaps nowhere more visibly than in India. The four Dharmic religions – Hinduism, Buddhism, Sikhism, and Jainism – tend to promote (though only Jainism requires) vegetarian diets. Hinduism also values *ahiṃsā,* or nonviolence, though not all adherents chose to observe strict vegetarianism; however, meat from the cow is forbidden. For Buddhists, vegetarian diets help them adhere to the First Precept which directs adherents to do no harm; some, such as Chinese Buddhist monks, have interpreted this to be a mandate to be vegetarian (Tseng, 2018). Finally, while there are some debates in Sikhism about whether followers must be vegetarian, text and teachings are clear that the Sikh community meal, or *langar*, must be vegetarian and that any meat that is consumed outside of the *langar* must not have a religious blessing (i.e., not be *halal* or *kosher*).

Still, it is difficult to find a religion that *preaches* unjustified violence. If nonviolence is a common value across religions, then why is vegetarianism not a common feature across religions? One alternative is to preach humane slaughter. While conceptions of what is "humane" have shifted over time with technological advances (Abdullah et al., 2019), the Prophet Muhammad commanded that slaughterers "should sharpen his knife, and let the slaughtered animal die comfortably" (Rahman, 2017). Though Muslims *can* eat meat, they must obtain that meat in nonviolent ways; a similar tradition has been passed down in the Jewish tradition of *shechita*. In sum, within a religious context, advocacy for a vegetarian lifestyle is often justified through principles of nonviolence. Even in cases where meat is okay, some religions may dictate rules for humane slaughter to minimize this violence.

3.7 Other Considerations

This is far from a definitive list of the intersection of food and religious values. Consider masculinity: As defined by Hofstede's cross-cultural work, the value of masculinity typically entails the realization of a few societal realities: patriarchal social hierarchies, larger gaps between men and women in assigned gender roles, and admiration for the physically and emotionally strong (Hofstede, 2001, 2011). How might masculinity play a role in food and religion? In 1982, Bruce Feirstein released a satire entitled "Real Men Don't Eat Quiche." This book prompted discussion around the feminization of certain foods such as quiche and vegetables (Cleves, 2022; Feirstein, 1982; Randall, 2016; Rothgerber, 2013; Rozin et al., 2012). But vegetarianism is a key or idealized feature of many world religions – do we see the same association between vegetables and femininity in these groups? Masculinity is just one underexplored value within religious food traditions. It is easy conceptualize how practices like mindful eating, vegetarianism, or food sharing promote values of reciprocity, harmony, and oneness. However, there is a severe lack of empirical and anthropological evidence of these values in play.

Another lingering empirical question within this space is the saliency of values when participating in traditions meant to reinforce them. How prominent is the idea of *ahiṃsā* in a Jain's day-to-day meals? Does engaging with these food traditions promote these values outside the food domain? If these traditions do not remind adherents of the values they are intended to promote, why do traditions persist?

Importantly, religious values may also be a way to promote social change. Vegetarianism is frequently prescribed within India's Dharmic religious groups, but adherence rate among Hindus is just 44 percent. Given that vegetarians have a dramatically reduced carbon foot compared to meat eaters, religion may provide a vector for promoting vegetarianism to reduce climate change, if it can be associated with existing religious values. One way to accomplish this is by leveraging the ethos of religious leaders. In another domain, vaccine-hesitant individuals were more likely to consider getting vaccinated if the message came from a religious leader, as opposed to other leaders (e.g., political leaders; Viskupič & Wiltse, 2022). Demonstrations by political leaders in line with religious values may also be powerful levers for change; Jain monks are known to protest animal slaughter in line with the principles of *ahimsa* (Evans, 2014). Therefore, if religious leaders can link core values to social action, we can leverage religion to promote positive change so long as we can do this in ways that respect the religions.

As with much of the research on food and religion, there is little exploration of the biopsychosocial mechanisms. As mentioned, fasting is related to greater mindfulness. But why? Is this due to positive emotions? The hormonal effects of fasting? Does *feast*ing decrease mindfulness? Without answers to mechanistic question about *how* food, religion, and values interact, we lack a full understanding of the phenomena.

Lastly, as we have seen with the Big Mac and Welch's grape juice, businesses are constantly interacting with religious values. As yet another example of the intersection of business, religion, and food, consider the Sanitas Nut Food Company, founded at the turn of the twentieth century. Guided by their Seventh-day Adventist values of healthy eating, brothers John and William founded a company which produced a wheat-based breakfast cereal. Today, that company is one of the largest cereal brands in the world – Kellogg – though the average consumer is likely unaware of the company's religious past. When enmeshed in religious values, how do companies maintain or move away from these values over time? How are these values communicated to consumers? How do consumers perceive religiously based companies selling secular products (like cereal)?

3.8 Conclusion

The study of values has produced a robust body of literature to borrow from. Still, there is more to be understood about how food comes to embody values and how salient these values are during meals. However, there is plentiful evidence that cleanliness, charity, mindfulness, thankfulness, and nonviolence play a crucial role in the consumption and preparation of food. As with the vegetarian diet of Sikhs, food more broadly is an excellent vessel to remind and teach us of what we really value.

4 Practices

Imagine you are out to dinner with your coworkers. As the server takes orders, you overhear your coworker, Sam, discreetly ask the waiter if the food is *halal* because he is Muslim. The waiter apologizes but states that their steakhouse does not carry *halal* meat. Sam states that it is fine and decides not to order anything, even though he told you earlier that he had skipped lunch and was quite hungry. How would you feel about Sam after watching this exchange?

When we asked participants in our lab about Sam, Muslims trusted Sam significantly more after he forewent food, relative to a control condition and to a condition in which Sam ordered a non-*halal* steak, despite the teachings of his religion. The most striking thing about this study was that even Christian participants trusted Sam more if, as a Muslim, he obeyed his dietary restrictions, which would presumably signal Sam's commitment to his own religion and other Muslims, but not to religious outsiders; instead, people seemed to see costly adherence to one's own religion, whatever that is, as a signal of trustworthiness (Hall et al., 2015). Sam engaged in what researchers call a costly signal – a sign of his dedication to his religion – and it improved other's impressions of him. And all he had to do was not order a steak.

When describing Islam, any definition of the religion would be remiss without accounting for the intricate systems of *halal* rules – prescriptions for what is good and pure, including food. The *halal* diet requires that animals be slaughtered in a humane way and that pork, pork byproducts, and alcohol be avoided. In addition to observing a *halal* diet, Muslims are called to fast from sunrise to sunset during the month of Ramadan. This practice, *sawm,* is the fourth pillar of Islam and is observed by an estimated 1.5 billion Muslims each year (Shatila et al., 2021). Depending on the time of year (as Ramadan follows the lunar, not Gregorian, calendar) and the location, fasting can last up to 20 hours. Traditionally, after the sun sets, the fast is broken with dates and water, followed by a larger meal. Perhaps, this goes for any religion – you cannot understand the religion if you do not understand how it thinks about food.

Food lies at the center of many religious practices which we will divide into: food prescriptions, food proscriptions, food preparation, and offerings. The importance of food in religious diets and ceremonies is due, in part, to its role in the beliefs and values previously discussed. In this section, we describe the many roles that food takes within daily religious life – from sacrifices to signaling – and why food is an ideal vector for this.

4.1 The Psychology of Practices

Religious practices are the actions and behaviors that religious adherents conduct as a part of their religious life. These include prayer, meditation, tithing, attending services, worship, sacrificing, and reading scripture. Certain practices may also be considered rituals– significant, scripted activities that adherents participate in to connect with other adherents and the divine (Bell, 1997). Hobson et al. (2018) specify that rituals must have a physical and psychological component, as well as a symbolic component to join the two. The authors provide an example of this: the *Seder* table. The *Seder* table is set during the Jewish holiday of Passover in a very specific way. In the Ashkenazi tradition, the plate contains six items:

1. *beitzah*: roasted egg
2. *chazeret*: lettuce or a bitter herb
3. *zaroa*: shank bone
4. *charoset*: mixture of fruits, nuts, and spices (though this varies by family and geography)

5. *karpas*: Parsley, to be dipped in salt water
6. *maror*: bitter herb, usually horseradish

The physical component of the *Seder* table is obvious: the plate and its components. The practice is psychologically, culturally, and religiously significant to practitioners; this practice means more to them than setting the table for a normal dinner. Lastly, the symbolic component is evident in the food choices. The bitter herbs symbolize how the Egyptians embittered the lives of the Hebrew slaves, the salt water or vinegar reminiscent of the tears of the enslaved Hebrews, the *charoset* symbolizing the mortar with which the slaves built, and so on.

Additionally, rituals are not arbitrary – they are deeply and inextricably entwined with values and beliefs that embolden them with significance. Consider communion – why bread and wine? Why not olives and honey? The bread and wine are intentional choices made to imitate the last meal of Christ (which was a traditional Passover meal). Thus, their significance is derived from mimicry of a higher power (a value that we should try to imitate God) and from Christ's instructions about how to take communion (a belief about the story of the first communion).

Religious practices have benefits beyond the realm of increasing one's faith (Stein et al., 2021). Religious rituals can increase our self-control (Kay et al., 2009; Koole et al., 2017), increase positive emotions (Van Cappellen et al., 2016), and create and strengthen interpersonal trust and social bonds (Hall et al., 2015; Sosis, 2004). Each of these benefits is apparent when considering meditation: a practice common in multiple religious and spiritual communities. One study found that a 6-week meditation intervention saw a significant reduction in stress and an increase in self-control (Canby et al., 2015). Further, meditations can be guided to elicit specific positive emotions, such as loving-kindness (Fredrickson et al., 2017). Lastly, in a lab context, such meditation boosted social connection with strangers (Hutcherson et al., 2008).

4.2 Food Prescriptions and Proscriptions

Food prescriptions describe the foods that members of a culture should eat. Some food prescriptions are linked to a person's status and may be the source of their status. For the general public, food prescriptions typically manifest as traditional foods tied to discrete moments in time. For example, in Christianity, the consumption of bread and wine is a religiously dictated prescriptive practice that only occurs in a specific context: the Eucharist. Some traditional foods, such as *gujiya*, a sweet pastry consumed during the Hindu festival of *Holi*, have a more lighthearted significance. The sweet pastry is meant to symbolize the sweetness of life and the joy embodied by the festival.

Food proscriptions, or food taboos, describe the foods that members of a cultural group should not eat. These are quite common – in one sample of historic and contemporary religious groups, 46 percent of religious groups had at least one tabooed food (Wormley & Cohen, 2022). Some food taboos are directed at a single food item. Other food taboos may ban an entire type of food – vegetarianism is practiced by Jains. *Kashrut*, the complex set of Jewish dietary laws, determine what is *kosher* ("acceptable") or not. In general, *kashrut* outlines which foods are acceptable or not (e.g., pork is not acceptable), how animals should be slaughtered in a specific, humane fashion, and specifies that dairy and meat should never mix, among many other requirements. However, *kashrut* has specific proscriptions as well: Jews cannot consume the sciatic nerve or blood vessels around it, or grape products made by non-Jewish individuals. Importantly, not all communities or adherents of a religion may adhere to proscriptions in the same way, based on individual interpretations or specific sects. For example, the prohibition of grape products made by non-Jewish individuals is typically only observed by Orthodox Jews.

Food taboos may also be contextually applied, depending on the characteristics of an individual (e.g., pregnant or lactating; Henrich & Henrich, 2010; Meigs, 1978). In the Orang Asli tribes of Malaysia, members believe that all animals have spirits. When an animal is consumed, the spirit of the human must battle with the spirit of the animal. As a result, only adults are capable of battling (and consuming) the spirits of larger game, such as monkeys, deer, and elephants. Thus, food is progressively tabooed depending on the size of the animal and the age of the person (Meyer-Rochow, 2009). These taboos in the Orang Asli also demonstrate the powerful role of symbolism in the role of food (see Section 3); this size of the animal symbolizes the size of their spirit which must be fought after consumption.

Taboos may also be justified as a way to practice avoiding temptations. Korean temple food, as described in Section 3, is free of pungent spices or smells (Park et al., 2020). This "bland" approach to food is designed to promote mindfulness, but it is also a powerful practice in self-control. Marshall (2010) suggests that the combination of temptation and tradition is what defines tabooed foods, writing:

> Objects acquire taboos when they elicit strong motivational states ("temptation"), which are suppressed by socially mediated and often unconscious forms of behavioral control ("tradition"), and the mind is left to rationalize the discrepancy by imposing moral judgments upon the objects of the behavior at hand, thereby "sacralizing" them. These in turn both justify the

abstinence (or the obligation), and make it easier to maintain. In short, the sacred is produced by the collision of temptation and tradition. (pp. 67–68)

When adherents obey food taboos, they are practicing self-control – which may benefit other domains of life, such as health (Miller et al., 2011). Religious people have better self-control (McCullough & Willoughby, 2009) and religious food rituals may be one important reason why.

While year-round food *pre*scriptions from religions are practically nonexistent, year-round food proscriptions are again, quite common. So why do religions focus on what adherents *cannot* eat rather than what they *can* eat? Here, we return to the idea of costly signaling: actions taken by an adherent that come at some detriment to them to demonstrate their commitment to the group or its moral code (Sosis, 2003). Research on costly signals, such as fasting or adhering to a strict diet (at the cost of foregone calories), has shown that this improves intra- and inter-group relationships by demonstrating trustworthiness (Northover et al., 2024). Singh and Henrich (2020) find that shamanic healers who observed multiple food taboos were seen as more cooperative, sincere in their faith, and supernaturally endowed.

For the average adherent, costly signals may also serve as a key to unlock the benefits of being a part of a group: shared resources, protection, information, co-parenting. Restricted diets, as shown by Hall and colleagues (2015), are one clear way to demonstrate one's commitment to their group. It would be more difficult for a religious group to identify a food item that (1) would come at a detriment (but not life-threatening) to the consumer and (2) encourage its consumption. Thus, religions may have evolved to be on the lookout for what to *ban* rather than what to *encourage*.

From a cultural evolution perspective, dietary restrictions may serve additional functional purposes beyond costly signaling. There have been some musings that food taboos within culture and religion are due to disease threat (Albright, 1994; Chandler and Read, 1961; Douglas, 2003; Golden and Comaroff, 2015; Gould, 1970; Meyer-Rochow, 2009; Simoons, 1994) though our own work shows no systematic link between the two (Wormley & Cohen, 2022). Similarly, taboos may be levied against unhealthy or deadly foods, such as toxic marine species for pregnant or breastfeeding women (Henrich & Henrich, 2010) or alcohol (as seen in many Christian sects, Buddhism, and the Bahá'í Faith). Lastly, some have proposed that food taboos may be an environmental management strategy (Meyer-Rochow, 2009). For example, Colding and Folke (1997) argue food taboos arise in response to scarcity within the environment, as evidence by the fact that approximately 30 percent of food taboos prohibit the consumption of species that are listed as endangered. Chiefs and priests within traditional Hawaiian culture might also place a temporary taboo on a food item if it was scarce (O'Connor, 2008).

4.3 Fasting

Fasting represents a unique form of food proscriptions: a temporary ban on all (or most) foodstuffs and/or liquids. Fasting is the defined, intentional, purposive abstinence from eating or drinking, which is often undertaken for spiritual or ritual purposes, in many faith traditions (Akram, 2016). Many religions require or promote this practice. In the Eastern Orthodox Church, there are anywhere from 180 to 200 days each year that require fasting (Trepanowski & Bloomer, 2010). In the Bahá'í faith, fasting is a nineteen-day-long practice beginning at sunset on March 1 and ending at sunset on March 20 marking the start of the new Bahá'í calendar year. As discussed in Section 3, the Bahá'í practice of fasting is meant to promote mindfulness (Ring et al., 2022), with practitioners only eating from sunset to sunrise each day. Within the *Kitáb-i-Aqdas*, *Bahá'u'lláh*, the founder of the Bahá'í faith, writes that "Fasting is the supreme remedy and the most great healing for the disease of self and passion." As with most religions, the Bahá'í faith provides exemptions to fasting for the sick, young, elderly, or pregnant. Outside of holidays, religious fasting may be prescribed as a form of penance, as in medieval Catholicism (Tamney, 1986).

It is important to note that these practices are not always a "complete fast" and may target specific foods. For example, the Daniel Fast, promoted by Christian groups including Seventh-day Adventists and Catholics, mimics Daniel's twenty-one days of fasting in the Bible. As a part of the fast, practitioners avoid meat, alcohol, and rich foods while focusing on fruits, vegetables, and healthy grains. Historically, Catholics abstain from eating meat on Fridays during the Lenten period, though fish is permitted. This exception has given way to traditions such as "Friday Fish Fries," which are common in the Midwest to raise money for churches. The Catholic Church has also declared amphibians and reptiles to be okay, allowing for the consumption of alligator and iguana in some Catholic communities (Bunderson, 2013; Fitch & Henderson, 2003). Yet another example of a partial fast, in the *Anishinaabe* culture, young girls refrain from eating berries for a year at the onset of their first menstrual cycle as they make the transition into womanhood; the end of that year is marked by a feast involving berries (LaPier, 2020).

What are the effects of fasting? Although fasting can have both negative (Leiper et al., 2003; Urkin & Naimer, 2015) and positive physical health implications (Tinsley & La Bounty, 2015), fasting can also have positive psychological outcomes such as increased cooperation (Bayani et al., 2020;

Crane, 2017; Rad, 2023). Fasting requires self-control, which is also linked with the virtues of humility (Tong et al., 2016) and generosity (Ugur, 2021). There is also some emerging evidence to suggest that fasting may improve mood in patients with psychiatric disorders or chronic pain (Fond et al., 2013; Michalsen, 2010; Stapel et al., 2022). Further, there appear to be spiritual benefits to fasting; Bahá'í who participated in intermittent dry fasting reported an increase in religiosity and mindfulness during the fasting period (Demmrich et al., 2021). Thus, fasting may be a means of enacting one's religious values while also experiencing physical, mental, and spiritual benefits. However, it is important to note that many of these studies focus on complete fasts – rather than partial fasts.

4.4 Preparation

In addition to the food item itself, the ritual preparation and consumption of food may be significant. Ritual preparation is almost always about maintaining purity – a common value across religious groups (see Section 3). For example, to maintain the purity of meat, the method of slaughter in the kosher tradition requires slaughtering in a swift, smooth cut of a sharp, perfect blade without hesitation (Appel, 2016). This method is also meant to be a reflection of one's humanity and a maintenance of humility, gratefulness, mindfulness, and self-control. A space may also need to be ritually prepared. Before Passover, Jewish houses must remove all traces of *chametz* – or leavened products – before Passover. Lastly, a person may need to undergo ritual cleansing. Before attending a Buddhist tea ceremony, attendees should wash in a *tsukubai*, or a stone basin with a ladle. Alternatively, a "cleansed person" may refer to someone who is spiritually clean, such as a nun; Korean temple food should be prepared by Buddhist nuns.

Preparation of food may also be a mental task. In addition to maintaining a clean workspace, adherents may also need to keep a clean mind and focus on pure thoughts. While preparing food for deities, cooks in Hindu temples might chant "*Hare Krishna*", as a way to keep their mind clear of impure thoughts. The importance of physical and spiritual clean food is underscored in the Chandogya Upanishad: "When food is pure, the mind becomes pure; when the mind is pure, remembrance becomes steady." Mindfulness while cooking is documented in other religions as well, such as Zen Buddhism ("Handle even a single leaf of green in such a way that it manifests the body of the Buddha" from *Tenzo Kyokun*) and Christianity ("So whether you eat or drink or whatever you do, do it all for the glory of God" from 1 Corinthians 10:31).

Ritual preparation of food plays a noticeably important role in the Lucumí tradition (also known as Santería). Novices spend a considerable amount of time in the kitchen, preparing food for fellow adherents and for divine sacrifice. This practice serves multiple purposes including demonstrating one's commitment to the faith, gaining exposure to the beliefs and values of the community, practicing self-discipline, and developing ritual competence. As Pérez (2011) observes, "cooking, seemingly the lowliest of undertakings in a Lucumí house, has been essential for the internalization of dispositions and relationships to the orishas that lead to initiation" (p. 673).

4.5 Offerings

Offerings to divinity or deceased ancestors play a critical role in many of the world's religions. In some traditions, offering food is seen as a sign of respect to the recipient (Grapard, 2021), in others, food may literally feed the recipient (O'Connor, 2008). After the offering ritual, food may be consumed by the offerer, burnt, donated to priests or monks, or left behind (Beerden, 2012). Offerings may be offered continuously, on specific auspicious days, to offer thanks for a bountiful harvest, or to placate an angry spirit (Brumberg-Kraus, 2024). The Hollyhock Ritual Festivity, performed on May 15 each year, began in the Shinto tradition to end a divine punishment that brought about a season of bad crops in the sixth century (Breen, 2020). At one shrine alone, a three-course meal is presented, consisting of dumplings, mochi, kelp, sweet potatoes, rice brew, cooked rice, cod broth, fruit, vegetables, thirteen varieties of seafood, multiple cakes, and chestnuts (Grapard, 2021). In the Candomblé religion, dishes such as *acaçá,* soaked and ground corn wrapped in banana leaves, are offered to *orixás*, or deities, to provide them with *axé*, a sacred lifeforce (Souza, 2015).

Little work has been done on the psychological effects of offerings, especially offering food. However, research has documented that visiting shrines increases self-reported positive emotions and mood (Canel-Çınarbaş et al., 2013; Charan et al., 2018). In addition to emotional benefits, we might expect that offerings enhance social connections among coreligionists, as well as increasing connections between the offerer and the spiritual world. Thus, the effects of religious offerings on behavior and cognition are a significant conceptual hole and are rather important, given that offerings play a major role in Hinduism, Taoism, Zoroastrianism, Buddhism, Shintoism, Judaism, and many indigenous religious traditions.

4.6 Open Questions

Religious practices have many noted benefits. However, perhaps few have been tested directly with rituals surrounding food. For example, Hall et al. (2015) test the idea that adhering to religious food taboos boost trust within the in-group and, probably more surprisingly, the out-group. But does adhering to religious food taboos increase positive emotions, similarly to how engaging in ritual worship seemingly does? Does adhering to religious food taboos increase self-control as "religiousness" in general does (McCullough & Willoughby, 2009)? There is reason to think that different rituals have different benefits, thus necessitating a wide variety of rituals for an individual to receive all of these benefits. Future work may attempt to explain *why* some outcomes are related to some rituals but not others or whether they are effective when administered as an intervention.

Additional work is needed to connect religious practices to broader theories. In an excellent review on religious dietary practices, Arslan and Aydin (2024) connect adherence to religious dietary laws to social identity theory and cognitive dissonance theory. Here, the authors argue that obeying religious dietary laws allows individuals to act on their religious identity and demonstrate one's role within the religious community. However, other pressures (e.g., hunger, other social identities) may lead to conflict between one's religious identity and these additional factors. While promising, more research should be done on religious food practices within the bounds and methods of established theories.

In existing work, and perhaps in our own description of food practices, there is an assumption of within-group homogeneity. However, religious practices can be extremely varied, even within a particular sect or geographic region. Buddhism consists of three main traditions (e.g., Mahayana, Vajrayana, and Theravada), each with dozens of smaller sects or schools. Buddhists are united in their pursuit of the Four Noble Truths and the Eight-fold Path, but differ in *what* is emphasized and *how* one should practice. Chinese Mahayana Buddhists tend to observe vegetarianism and it is required for those in monastic life, but lay practitioners and monastics in the Theravada tradition are not beholden to vegetarianism (Kieschnick, 2005; Tseng, 2018). Additionally, Jews of Eastern European descent (Ashkenazic Jews) have many different Passover traditions than do Jews of Spanish and North African descent (Sephardic Jews). For example, Sephardic Jews consume rice and legumes on Passover, and Ashkenazic Jews do not. Differences in religious food practices exist within arguably every religious group. This should caution researchers to not make assumptions about participants when conducting research, but may also prove to be a fruitful path of inquiry: Where and why do within-group differences in religious food practices come about?

4.7 Conclusion

Practices surrounding food in religion often embody the beliefs and values previously discussed in this Element. From restrictions to offerings, religious food practices are incredibly diverse. As an observable behavior which embodies the previously discussed beliefs and values, religious practices should be especially interesting to social scientists. However, our understanding of the effects of religious practices on affect, cognition, and other downstream behaviors is sorely lacking.

5 Community

For a free meal, one need only turn to a *gurdwara*, or a Sikh temple. Volunteers prepare and serve meals out of an attached community kitchen, called a *langar*, driven by the Sikh value of *seva*, or selfless service. The meals are vegetarian (though there is no mandate in Sikhism to be vegetarian) so that the meals might be more accessible to those with varying dietary restrictions. The meals are funded purely by donations. Depending on the temple, food may even be available 24/7 and is open to anyone – even non-Sikhs – regardless of their background with no expectations of conversion. All guests eat the same meal on the ground – a reminder of the equality of all humans – and a way to overcome the boundaries of caste.

On the day our research team visited, we were greeted with a spread of food: chickpea salad, chutneys, pasta, and chai. This buffet had been prepared for the volunteers preparing food for that evening's dinner and the larger meal to be served the next morning. After observing evening services, we were ushered back downstairs for another meal: dal, rice, salad, *seviyan* (a vermicelli pudding), and *chapati* (unleavened flatbread), served by circulating volunteers out of buckets with ladles. In the back of the kitchen, a group of students from a nearby university continued preparing for the next morning's meal under the watchful eyes of more experienced "aunties." Over the sink, a list of rules for the kitchen reminded volunteers to mentally recite "*Waheguru*" – which figuratively translates to "Wonderful God" – while working.

During the COVID-19 pandemic, the dynamics of the *langar* had to change. Need was greater, as many individuals struggled with food insecurity during the pandemic, but stay-at-home orders and social distancing made the typical *langar* meal tricky. Some *gurdwaras* delivered meals to individuals at home, while others doubled down on efforts to build food pantries. But communities from Glasgow, Scotland to Phoenix, Arizona (where one *langar* operates out of a food truck) to Amritsar, India (which serves over 50,000 meals a day) have reported that these meals make a difference in the lives of thousands.

It is no surprise that food brings us together, even outside of religious contexts: Sunday family meals, anniversary dinners at Michelin star restaurants, and work picnics. But the *langar* embodies the unique ability of food to bring people from different cultural and religious identities together and create any easy point of connection. At the gurdwara we visited, they expected approximately 350 visitors on any given Sunday – approximately 50 of them will be unaffiliated with Sikhism. However, we can also imagine that for co-religionists, these shared meals strengthen one's connection to the religious community. One might find themselves eating on the floor next to their neighbor, a complete stranger, a picky three-year-old, a first-generation, elderly immigrant from Punjab, or a team of curious researchers. While chopping vegetables and making *chapati*, the volunteers at the *langar* might seek counsel about spiritual troubles, discuss upcoming holidays, and build friendships across generations.

Thus far, we have discussed how food plays a role in three components of religion: beliefs, values, and practices. The final component of religion is the community shared between co-religionists. Food plays a central role in building this community for many faiths. Food can be a way to share and reinforce the community's history. Communal meals and food sharing are often viewed as a bonding mechanism which promotes cooperation – and may be a tool for proselytizing. Here, we reflect on the many ways that food contributes to community building, and the important role that community plays in eliciting the benefits of religion.

5.1 The Psychology of Community

Within religion, community describes the social aspect of religious life, including how adherents bond with one another and develop a shared collective identity (Saroglou et al., 2020). Given that approximately 84 percent of the world's population identifies as religiously affiliated (Pew Research Center, 2012), most individuals are a part of a religious community that may span continents. For example, as the world's fifth largest religion, with over 25 million adherents, Sikh *gurdwaras* exist on every continent except Antarctica. The world's fastest growing religion, Islam, is projected to have 2.76 billion adherents in 2050 (Wormald, 2015).

Discussion of communities also requires a discussion of where such communities meet. Of course, places of worship are a common feature of many religions – temples, churches, synagogues, cathedrals, mosques, gurdwaras, monasteries, shrines, or adherents' homes. For the 3.48 million Muslims in America in 2010, there were 2,106 mosques (Bagby, 2020; Wormald, 2015). Importantly, many of these places feature kitchens for cooking communal meals. Such kitchens serve a purpose beyond cooking; Pérez (2016) argues that the activities taking place in these kitchens – chopping, simmering, sauteing, and serving – provide cooks "with the repertoire of skills, dispositions, and habits necessary for religious norms to be internalized." In the age of the internet, these places need not be physical. Religious communities may converge on blogsites, Facebook pages, or Zoom calls (Campbell, 2011). These virtual spaces may also facilitate sharing religiously significant recipes, cooking tutorials, and meal trains.

Importantly, being a part of a religious community provides sources of social support, which in turn predict better physical and mental health (Koenig et al., 1997). Social support is the "perception or experience that one is cared for, esteemed, and part of a mutually supportive social network" (Taylor, 2011, p. 189) and comes in many forms. For example, from one's religious community, an individual can obtain informational support (e.g., "There is a new *halal* grocer down the road"), functional support (e.g., food from bishops' storehouses in LDS communities), or companionate support (e.g., shared meals following religious services). Likely as a result of these many forms of social support, religious individuals tend to be less anxious (Whitehead, 2018), less depressed (Ai et al., 2013), and drink alcohol less (Holt et al., 2018). That religiosity is linked to greater social support and improved health can help explain the fact that religious individuals tend to live longer than their non-religious counterparts (McCullough et al., 2000, 2009; Wallace et al., 2019).

5.2 Communal History

Food is one of the major ways in which communities relive their shared histories, the community's shared cycles, and shared community traditions (Cohen, 2021). When it comes to shared history, for example, on the Jewish new year, *Rosh Hashanah*, apples and honey (sometimes, pomegranates) are eaten to usher in a sweet year, and on the new year for trees, *Tu Bishvat*, various fruits and nuts are eaten. Shared history may also be commemorated via fasting such as on Yom Kippur where Jews communally atone for the sins committed by members of the community. Fasting may also be used to mark historical events, as on *Tisha b'Av*, to mourn the destruction of the Temples in Jerusalem in 130 BCE and 70 CE.

Examples of food representing a slice of a religion's history can be found around the world. The weekly partaking of the Eucharist is a reliving of the Last Supper, and Easter, also a springtime holiday, celebrates new transitions and rebirth, much as does the Passover *seder*; both incorporate eggs in this symbolic way. For Buddhist monks today, eating what food laypeople provide via alms is an imitation of the tradition of the Buddha and his disciples relying on donations from others to eat.

5.3 Communal Meals

The *Last Supper* by Leonardo da Vinci depicts one of the most famous communal meals worldwide. Jesus sits at the center of a long table with His twelve disciples distributed on either side of Him. In this dramatic moment, over scattered loaves of bread and glasses of wine, Jesus announces that one of the dinner party attendees will betray Him. In addition to being an act of community building, this meal represents a critical turning point within Christianity and is immortalized in practices such as communion. Communal meals like the Last Supper are common across religious communities. The Last Supper itself was likely held during the Jewish holiday of Passover (Jeremias, 1949).

Shared meals vary in how structured they are. For example, Passover represents a highly structured meal. As noted in Section 4, what is eaten, how it is eaten, and when it is eaten indicates that the Passover meal is a ritualistic practice, the order of which is highly prescribed and recited throughout the *seder* (in fact, the very word *seder* means "order"). In contrast, *langars* follow general guidelines (e.g., the meal should be vegetarian), but can vary significantly from day-to-day and temple-to-temple. Additionally, coreligionists may share meals outside of formal practices; a men's Bible study may meet at an IHOP for breakfast and fellowship.

The benefits of eating meals together – in secular or religious contexts – are well documented in the scientific literature. In the UK, individuals who frequently had dinner with others tended to be happier, more trusting, and felt as though they had more social support (Dunbar, 2017). For the elderly, who are prone to undereating, sharing meals is associated with more food intake (Paquet et al., 2008), and within families, children who had more family meals tended to eat healthier, by way of increased self-regulation (De Wit et al., 2015). Thus, we should expect (though empirical evidence is limited) that communal meals within religious contexts boost physical and mental health, potentially by way of increased feelings of social support and enhanced self-regulation.

5.4 Community beyond the Faith

Critically, food need not be only used in building connections within one's religion – it is an important tool for connecting with those outside the faith. Perhaps the most notable feature of the *langar* is that it is open to anyone, regardless of faith, and does not involve efforts to convert attendees to Sikhism. The principle motivation for *langars* is to practice selfless service toward everyone. Hinduism offers a similar message of hospitality (Lashley & Lashley, 2016); adherents are taught that an "uninvited guest should be treated as good as God" and "even an enemy must be offered appropriate hospitality if he comes to your home. A tree does not deny its shade even to the one who has come to cut it down." Here, we can see that food is taught to be a means for building connections beyond co-religionists – perhaps even among enemies.

Communal meals may also create a venue for religions to gain followers. For example, the charity work of the Church World Service began following the Second World War when famine ravaged much of Europe and Asia (Church World Service, n.d.). While the organization donated millions of pounds of food to these regions, they also engaged in missionary work – rebuilding churches that had previously been destroyed and introducing new ones in previously untouched regions. The food provided the initial connection between humanitarian relief, but their promotion materials also argued that beneficiaries "hungered" for the religious message as well. God and "the Truth" were "as important as bread" in these regions. Indeed, this strategy proved effective. Along with relief work in Pakistan, one CWS preacher accomplished over 500 baptisms in five years (Church World Service, 1925). While soup kitchens and food drives may indeed represent sincere efforts to embody values such charity, they also represent an opportunity to convert individuals into the faith, thus growing the religious community.

It is important to note that there are certainly ethical concerns surrounding the role of food in proselytization. For all the power food has to unite us, it can also be a devastating tool. One Native American elder remarked that, "Religion really had a lot to do with foods on the reservation when we became Christianized and baptized. One way to get the people to come to church was to feed them. The nuns and the priests would feed the people. If you would not get baptized, they would not feed you. It was always a threat" (Colby et al., 2012, p. 69). In recognition of the harm this causes, many religious groups denounce these practices; a 2011 interfaith commission of Christian churches stated that "If Christians engage in inappropriate methods of exercising mission [bearing witness] by resorting to deception and coercive means, they betray the gospel and may cause suffering to others." Of course, not all efforts to share food across faith lines are coercive; many are rooted in sincerity.

This is evidence by communal interfaith meals that have no intention of proselytization at all. Similar to the langar, the Passover *seder* promises, "all who are hungry, let them come and eat"; some communities make it a practice to invite both Jews and Gentiles. Given that both Sikhism and Judaism do not encourage proselytization, this promise to feed everyone, regardless of their religious background is interesting. Despite a lack of *active* efforts to convert attendees, these meals provide a chance to learn about a religion and observe its values at play; if these features appeal to an attendee, it may encourage them to consider converting.

5.5 Other Considerations

Religion is broadly understood to be beneficial for one's mental and physical health, in large part due to the social support it offers. While it is often theorized that religion's effects on health are partly explained by social support and healthy lifestyles (Cohen & Koenig, 2003), more formal tests of these links – and how the context of food matters – would be valuable. Presently, there is an obvious need for a study which tests the causal, mediational link between religious life, social support, and health in a broad, representative sample. Existing work may address one facet of religious life (e.g., religious attendance; Ai et al., 2013) or may only look at a specific population (e.g., African Americans; Holt et al., 2018). Similar treatment is needed to understand the role of food in the relationship between religion and health (Purnell & Jenkins, 2013). For example, separate bodies of literature suggest that communal meals promote health outcomes in secular settings (Dunbar, 2017; Stockbridge et al., 2023), but this work has not tested potential mechanisms (e.g., feelings of social support, healthier eating habits) or explored whether religious social contexts provide convey additional benefits. These relations may indeed be moderated by group memberships for a variety of reasons, such as predispositions to varying health conditions, varying importance of religion, and the role of food in religious life.

It remains an interesting and unexplored empirical question about how much language vs. appearance vs. food traditions are seen to constitute and differentiate religious communities. As previously mentioned, Sephardic and Ashkenazic Jews vary in their Passover traditions, among many other aspects of religious and secular life. How are these differences viewed *within* broad religious traditions? How much do Sephardic Jews think it is silly to avoid rice or peas on Passover, or how much do Ashkenazic Jews think it is lackadaisical to eat them? Or do people see these groups' differences as equally valid ways of honoring one's obligation to commemorate Passover? Further, how are differences in diet perceived between religious communities? Do vegetarian Buddhists see meat eaters of other religions as being just as moral, and it is only incumbent upon one's own group to observe the group's food rules? Or do people think certain rules really ought to be universally observed? Do Jews or Muslims think it's fine for others not to keep *kashrut* or observe *halal* rules? Or that everyone should?

Lastly, as we have demonstrated, food is a powerful medium for connecting individuals both within and between religious faiths. However, not every individual or religion is accepting of interfaith dining. Perhaps these different beliefs about interfaith dining are predictive of other, broader views toward outgroups.

5.6 Conclusion

Despite William James' (James, 1902) hesitance to include it in his definition of religion, the last component of religion – community – is truly a critical characteristic; to be religious is to join a community that shares your beliefs, values, and practices. Food can help bring these groups together and, via active or passive efforts to convert, help religions grow. Food is also a tool for reflecting on communal history through symbolism and ritualistic preparation and consumption. Still, we understand little about how religious food practices serve to define and differentiate religious groups and how perceptions of food practices may influence broader perceptions of a religious group.

6 Conclusion

The study of food shows how examining everyday practices can advance psychological theory and our understanding of religion. Far from trivial, this work has contributed to existing theories of human behavior, such as costly signaling and social identity theory. As an added bonus for the researcher, this space often contains an element of fun: trying new foods to properly understand one's subjects. While we have outlined open questions for the psychology of religion and food in each section, we close with three additional considerations for researchers to consider in the hope of encouraging more research within this space.

6.1 Substance Use

Thus far, this Element has focused largely on consumables that have no apparent psychoactive properties – what we call food. This leaves out a large, but important, aspect of religious life: the controversial role of alcohol, drugs, and psychoactive ingredients. There is significant variation in attitudes toward substance use, even within religious traditions. In the Church of Jesus Christ of Latter-day Saints, coffee – which contains caffeine – is banned under a general prohibition against hot drinks. Meanwhile, some evangelical churches have coffee shops on their grounds. Tobacco is used in rituals within American indigenous traditions, but Sikhism and Seventh-day Adventists explicitly ban its use. What can we learn about religion from the use and prohibition of these substances?

First, it is important to note that substance use within religious contexts has and continues to be a controversial topic. The use of psychoactive drugs in religious rituals, as exemplified by the case of *Employment Division v. Smith*, has been a source of significant public controversy. In 1963, the US Supreme Court held that it violated the First Amendment for the government to withhold unemployment benefits for a Seventh-day Adventist because she refused to work on Saturdays (*Sherbert v. Verner*, 526). This standard – that the government could not substantially burden a citizen's right to free exercise of religion – basically held until 1990, when the Court held that Native Americans could not use generally illegal peyote for religious purposes (*Employment Div., Dept. Of Human Resources of Ore. V. Smith*, 1989), holding that the free exercise of religion did not allow people to violate generally applicable laws.

Despite modern controversy, the use of psychoactive substances in religion is quite ancient. The historic Oracle at Delphi, under the guidance of the Greek God of Apollo, received prophetic visions of the future from a restricted *adyton* section of the temple. Now, scholars understand that the *adyton* was located atop geological fault that released ethylene. When inhaled, this sweet-smelling gas causes a trance-like state and powerful hallucinations – which might explain the Oracle's visions (Hale et al., 2003).

Today, exact numbers on the usage of illicit substances in religious rituals are nonexistent. But some 300,000 people follow the Native American Church which uses ritualistic *peyote*, 700,000 people are Rastafarian which promotes the usage of cannabis, and for over 900,000 Fijians, *kava* – a sedative drink – is an important part of social and spiritual life (Tomlinson, 2007). Thus, while rare in Western religions, the use of psychoactive substances for religious or spiritual reasons is not uncommon.

Historically, within psychological science, the use of substances in religion has gone understudied. This might be attributed to a host of factors including a tendency to focus on mainstream Abrahamic religions (which tend to discourage substance use, especially to excess) and ethical and legal concerns surrounding the study of illicit substances. Nevertheless, substances like alcohol and psychoactive drugs have played an important role in shaping religious practices and building communities.

Now, research on the effects of psychedelics is growing in popularity. Relevant to the study of religion, some users report spiritual experiences following psychedelic usage. In a recent review of thirty-four studies on the topic, one team of researchers reported that psychedelic usage was related to spiritual growth, which included "stronger perceived connections with the divine, a greater sense of meaning, increased spiritual faith, increased engagement in religious and spiritual practices, an increase in feelings of unity and self-transcendence, positive changes in worldview, increased connectedness with others, and reduced fear of death" (Schutt et al., 2024, p. 26372). However, individual differences in users' motivation are unclear; how often do individuals use psychedelics with the intention of having a spiritual experience? Further, what effects do psychedelics have on religiosity, especially its extrinsic components (e.g., religious service attendance)?

This space would benefit greatly from longitudinal research to determine (1) what motivates individuals to consume psychedelics (or not) and (2) how religious beliefs and values change over the course of psychedelic consumption. For example, researchers might place ads for individuals intending to use psychedelics for the first time and administer questionnaire pre-/post-consumption. As this body of research continues to grow, we would encourage these scholars to attend to the role religious and spiritual life might play in the use of psychoactive substances.

6.2 The Nonreligious

There is a growing movement within the psychology of religion to study phenomenon surrounding the nonreligious. Though 84 percent of the world still identifies as religiously affiliated, there is a growing number of individuals who do not identify as religiously affiliated. However, this group is far from homogenous. The religiously unaffiliated may still believe in God or a higher power (as is common in China), may identify as "spiritual but not religious" (SBNR), or may disavow both spiritual and religious beliefs. They may also be disillusioned with "organized religion" but still believe in a higher power. The religiously unaffiliated may further identity as atheist, agnostic, humanist, or another term to denote their specific beliefs.

Despite this diversity in what it means to be "nonreligious," what role might food play in the lives on the nonreligious? As the number of religiously unaffiliated people continues to grow, so does the research on this demographic. One thing we know is individuals that once identified as religious carry "religious residue" (Van Tongeren et al., 2021). Perhaps this residue extends to what foods they prefer or avoid. If an Orthodox Jew becomes secular, do they still avoid pork, or is the first thing they do is run out to a Mexican restaurant for *carne adovada*? Do former Jains indulge in meat products or maintain their vegetarian lifestyles? Does it depend on the religion (e.g., ex-Muslims are more likely to observe *halal* than ex-Jews observing *kosher*)? As with Muslims and Protestants in the "Sam" experiment from Section 4, do the nonreligious trust religious individuals who engage in costly signaling more than those who do not? Does this depend on whether one was *ever* religious or *never* religious, which religion they belonged to, or other cultural and contextual differences and individual characteristics?

However, research on the nonreligious may be complicated given that the religiously unaffiliated do not have the same binding beliefs, values, practices, and community that define religious life. Instead of pursuing quantitative, empirical questions, it may be best to pursue descriptive, ethnographic studies of the nonreligious for the time being. Admittedly, food may not play the same role in the lives of the nonreligious as it does the religious. Yet, we should attend to other ways that the nonreligious make meaning, form traditions, and make decisions around food; perhaps this is supplemented by other forms of culture (e.g., national identity, gender).

6.3 Etiology of Religion

In 1963, Niko Tinbergen posed four non-mutually contradictory questions to fully explore a behavior at multiple levels of analysis: (1) What is the functional significance of a behavior? (2) By what processes did that behavior come to be? (3) What directly causes the behavior? and (4) How does the behavior vary over the lifespan (Tinbergen, 1963)? If we want to truly understand religion, especially as it pertains to food, Tinbergen's four questions must be answered – yet existing research appears to lack in this domain.

To illustrate our point, we will answer Tinbergen's four questions in the context of religious food taboos. As discussed in Section 4, food proscriptions are common in many religious communities. Multiple functional explanations have been proposed but these functional explanations do and should vary in their level of analysis. Additionally, as researchers, we should pay more attention to different levels of mechanism when describing effects. One might take an individual-level approach: food taboos are a show of dedication to the group which reaps benefits beyond the costs of forgoing a particular food item. Alternatively, one could look at the collective-level; food taboos exist, so, as a collective, religious groups can manage limited resources by way of food taboos levied against endangered species. In sum, there are multiple, noncompeting explanations for the function of religious food taboos at different levels of analysis – and potentially more lay in wait.

Tinbergen's second question asks how natural selection may play a role in food taboos. Here, we might consider the emotion of disgust. Disgust is elicited in response to stimuli we find aversive, especially those relating to moral violations, pathogens, or sexual activity (Tybur et al., 2009). Anthropological accounts support the idea that when a food is tabooed, individuals tend to find it disgusting (Fessler & Navarrete, 2003) – even if it is a food that is otherwise tempting.

However, a more nuanced approach to this question is needed. Across religious groups, do we find that disgust, one of the most basic emotions (Rozin et al., 1994), is an adherent's first emotional response to a tabooed food? It is feasible, especially if taking the view that food taboos arise on desirable foods (e.g., pork, garlic), that disgust is not an automatic but learned response that may be secondary to initial desire. How do cultural learning processes play a role in developing a disgust response to a tabooed food? At what age do individuals develop an instinctual disgust response to a tabooed food? What foods are most tabooed: naturally tempting ones (as a way to demonstrate one's self-control) or naturally disgusting ones (as a way to avoid unsafe foods)? More generally, what is the driving force: evolved preferences or cultural taboos (or their interaction)? Further, we now understand that natural selection is just one form of selective pressure on human behavior. Genes and culture evolve alongside each other (Abdellaoui, 2022; Chiao & Blizinsky, 2010; Uchiyama et al., 2021); how might religious food prohibitions lead to genomic changes that transmit across generations (e.g., an inability to process meat proteins in the religiously vegetarian; Beja-Pereira et al., 2003; Perry et al., 2007)?

Religion presents a particular challenge for researchers interested in establishing causality and mechanisms (Moon et al., 2023). Since we cannot randomly assign participants to a religious affiliation, we must get creative in how we study the effects of religion on our psychology (e.g., longitudinal studies). In Section 5, we discussed how religious individuals tend to be healthier and live longer (Holt et al., 2018; Koenig et al., 1997; McCullough et al., 2000, 2009) – but the mechanisms underpinning this process are still not entirely clear and could benefit from more sustained attention – perhaps in the domain of food. Food may be one explanation for longer lives among the religious. Adhering to religious diets may promote avoidance of unhealthy foods (e.g., alcohol) which leads to longer lives (Ekmekcioglu, 2020; Fontana & Partridge, 2015). Evidence for this is seen in the Mormon community; in Utah, members of the

LDS community, who ought not to consume alcohol or tobacco, tend to live longer than non-LDS (Merrill, 2004). Similarly, longitudinal studies of Seventh-day Adventist show they tend to live longer (Fraser & Shavlik, 2001), likely due in part to the religion's promotion of a vegetarian and healthy lifestyle (Orlich et al., 2013). Religious communities create opportunities for communal meals, which can promote healthier eating (De Wit et al., 2015). These are two of many potential mechanisms (i.e., fasting; Persynaki et al., 2017), but robust tests of these and other mechanisms are lacking. Moreover, we should also be conscious of the fact that traditions surrounding food vary between religions, but even concrete tests of how longevity varies across religious affiliation are lacking (Sullivan, 2010).

Lastly, the role of religion over the lifespan is another area of research that is lacking. While research on levels of religiosity over the lifespan are numerous (McCullough et al., 2005), there is more to religious life than intensity of belief or religious service attendance. For example, in considering food taboos, how do individuals come to learn about these taboos over time? How does the disgust response to tabooed foods develop? Disgust responses can be observed in the lab via self-report, EEG, or facial expression (Robinson & Clore, 2002; Rozin et al., 1994; Sarlo et al., 2005) and correlated with participants' age to demonstrate how responses to tabooed foods vary over the life course.

6.4 Conclusion

We began this Element with the story of how McDonald's has adapted its highly successful business model to respect the beliefs and practices of religions around the globe. It is a powerful example of how religion and food come together to shape the world – but also what individuals, companies, and society stand to gain by understanding and respecting religious differences. The Big Mac is far from the only way religious food traditions have impacted secular life. The football Premier League has recently learned "to embrace" Ramadan and facilitates pre-arranged breaks for players who need to break their fasts during a game (Panja, 2024). Trader Joe's carries *latkes* – even after Hanukah. The BBC and *Vogue* magazine tout the benefits of *ghee* (Imtiaz, 2022; Signorelli, 2024). And Welch's Grape Juice – the company born out of a Protestant concern for consuming alcohol during communion – is a market leader. Thus, the study of food and religion goes beyond knowing ourselves and knowing others – it is also about learning to respect and enjoy what other religions have to offer. The menu is simply a palatable place to start.

References

ABC News. (2009, January 8). *Happy Birthday Big Mac*. https://abcnews.go.com/Business/story?id=3521002&page=1.

Abd Rahim, S., Mansor, S., Yakob, M. A., & Ismail, N. (2018). Food safety, sanitation and personal hygiene in food handling: An overview from Islamic perspective. *International Journal of Civil Engineering and Technology, 9*, 1524–1530.

Abdellaoui, A. (2022). The evolutionary dance between culture, genes, and everything in between. *Behavioral and Brain Sciences, 45*, e153. https://doi.org/10.1017/S0140525X2100176X.

Abdullah, F. A. A., Borilova, G., & Steinhauserova, I. (2019). Halal criteria versus conventional slaughter technology. *Animals, 9*(8), 530. https://doi.org/10.3390/ani9080530.

Ai, A., Huang, B., Bjorck, J., & Appel, H. (2013). Religious attendance and major depression among Asian Americans from a national database: The mediation of social support. *Psychology of Religion and Spirituality, 5*, 78–89. https://doi.org/10.1037/a0030625.

Akram, M. (2016). Meaning and significance of fasting in comparative perspective: A study with special reference to Judaism, Christianity, and Islam. *Hamdard Islamicus, 39*(2), 37–60.

Albright, W. F. (1994). *Yahweh and the Gods of Canaan: A Historical Analysis of Two Contrasting Faiths*. Eisenbrauns.

Amenga-Etego, R. M., Kwakye, A. N. O., Emeka-Nwobia, N., Onovoh, P., & Fretheim, S. (2021). Language, literature, prayer, and music repertoires as sources of African Christian spirituality and values. *International Bulletin of Mission Research, 45*(2), 111–120. https://doi.org/10.1177/2396939320961100.

Appel, G. (2016). *The Concise Code of Jewish Law: A Guide to the Observance of Shabbat*. Maggid.

Aquino, K., & Reed II, A. (2002). The self-importance of moral identity. *Journal of Personality and Social Psychology, 83*(6), 1423–1440. https://doi.org/10.1037/0022-3514.83.6.1423.

Arslan, S., & Aydın, A. (2024). Religious dietary practices: Health outcomes and psychological insights from various countries. *Journal of Religion and Health* 63, 3256–3273. https://doi.org/10.1007/s10943-024-02110-8.

Asi, L. N., Teri, D. T., & Meyer-Rochow, V. B. (2018). Influence of food taboos on nutritional patterns in rural communities in Cameroon. *International Review of Social Research, 8*(1), 2–6. https://doi.org/10.2478/irsr-2018-0013.

Badanta, B., Lucchetti, G., & de Diego-Cordero, R. (2020). "A temple of God": A qualitative analysis of the connection between spiritual/religious beliefs and health among Mormons. *Journal of Religion and Health*, *59*(3), 1580–1595. https://doi.org/10.1007/s10943-019-00922-7.

Bagby, I. (2020). *American Mosque Survey 2020 Report #1* (US Mosque Survey). https://ispu.org/report-1-mosque-survey-2020/.

Bardi, A., & Schwartz, S. H. (2003). Values and behavior: Strength and structure of relations. *Personality and Social Psychology Bulletin*, *29*(10), 1207–1220. https://doi.org/10.1177/0146167203254602.

Bayani, A. A., Esmaeili, R., & Ganji, G. (2020). The impact of fasting on the psychological well-being of Muslim graduate students. *Journal of Religion and Health*, *59*(6), 3270–3275. https://doi.org/10.1007/s10943-018-00740-3.

Beerden, K. (2012). It was divine... Gods and their food in the ancient Greek world. In McWilliams M. (Ed.), *Celebration: Proceedings of the Oxford Symposium of Food and Cookery 2011*. Totnes: Prospect Books, 49–55.

Beja-Pereira, A., Luikart, G., England, P. R. et al. (2003). Gene-culture coevolution between cattle milk protein genes and human lactase genes. *Nature Genetics*, *35*(4), 311–313. https://doi.org/10.1038/ng1263.

Bell, C. M. (1997). *Ritual: Perspectives and Dimensions*. Oxford University Press.

Boegershausen, J., Aquino, K., & Reed, A. (2015). Moral identity. *Current Opinion in Psychology*, *6*, 162–166. https://doi.org/10.1016/j.copsyc.2015.07.017.

Borré, K. (1991). Seal blood, Inuit blood, and diet: A biocultural model of physiology and cultural identity. *Medical Anthropology Quarterly*, *5*(1), 48–62. https://doi.org/10.1525/maq.1991.5.1.02a00080.

Breen, J. (2020). Performing history: Festivals and pageants in the making of modern Kyoto. In J. Breen, M. Hiroshi, & T. Hiroshi (Eds.), *Kyoto's Renaissance* (pp. 33–64). Amsterdam University Press. https://doi.org/10.1515/9781898823933-004.

Brook, D. (2009). The planet-saving mitzvah: Why Jews should consider vegetarianism. *Tikkun*, *24*(4), 29–73. https://doi.org/10.1215/08879982-2009-4012.

Brown, C. G. (2016). Can "secular" mindfulness be separated from religion? In R. E. Purser, D. Forbes, & A. Burke (Eds.), *Handbook of Mindfulness: Culture, Context, and Social Engagement* (pp. 75–94). Springer International. https://doi.org/10.1007/978-3-319-44019-4_6.

Brown, K. W., & Ryan, R. M. (2003). The benefits of being present: Mindfulness and its role in psychological well-being. *Journal of Personality and Social Psychology*, *84*(4), 822–848. https://doi.org/10.1037/0022-3514.84.4.822.

Brumberg-Kraus, J. (2012). Sukkot: The paradigmatic harvest festival. *Celebration: Proceedings of the Oxford Symposium of Food and Cookery 2011*. https://books.google.com/books?hl=en&lr=&id=wTwQDgAAQBAJ&oi=fnd&pg=PT55&dq=sukkot+paradigmatic&ots=9mCw34MJ4Y&sig=uKBVKeIuRGhzrRAC3OGFp6Fl8vk.

Brumberg-Kraus, J. (2024). Food and religious rituals. In *Oxford Research Encyclopedia of Food Studies*. https://oxfordre.com/foodstudies/display/10.1093/acrefore/9780197762530.001.0001/acrefore-9780197762530-e-21.

Bunderson, C. (2013, February 15). *Alligator OK to eat on Lenten Fridays, archbishop clarifies*. Catholic News Agency. www.catholicnewsagency.com/news/26593/alligator-ok-to-eat-on-lenten-fridays-archbishop-clarifies.

Butash, A. (2013). *Bless This Food: Ancient and Contemporary Graces from around the World*. New World Library.

Callahan, R. J., Lofton, K., & Seales, C. E. (2010). Allegories of progress: Industrial religion in the United States. *Journal of the American Academy of Religion*, 78(1), 1–39. https://doi.org/10.1093/jaarel/lfp076.

Campbell, H. (2011). Internet and religion. In Mia Consalvo & Charles Ess (Eds.). *The Handbook of Internet Studies* (pp. 232–250). John Wiley & Sons. https://doi.org/10.1002/9781444314861.ch11.

Canby, N. K., Cameron, I. M., Calhoun, A. T., & Buchanan, G. M. (2015). A brief mindfulness intervention for healthy college students and its effects on psychological distress, self-control, meta-mood, and subjective vitality. *Mindfulness*, 6(5), 1071–1081. https://doi.org/10.1007/s12671-014-0356-5.

Canel-Çınarbaş, D., Çiftçi, A., & Bulgan, G. (2013). Visiting shrines: A Turkish religious practice and its mental health implications. *International Journal for the Advancement of Counselling*, 35(1), 16–32. https://doi.org/10.1007/s10447-012-9162-8.

Chandler, A. C., & Read, C. P. (1961). *Introduction to parasitology* (Vol. 428). John Wiley & Sons New York.

Charan, I. A., Wang, B., & Yao, D. (2018). Cultural and religious perspective on the Sufi shrines. *Journal of Religion and Health*, 57(3), 1074–1094. https://doi.org/10.1007/s10943-018-0558-6.

Chiao, J. Y., & Blizinsky, K. D. (2010). Culture–gene coevolution of individualism–collectivism and the serotonin transporter gene. *Proceedings of the Royal Society B: Biological Sciences*, 277(1681), 529–537. https://doi.org/10.1098/rspb.2009.1650.

Church World Service. (n.d.). *CWS: A Brief History*. Retrieved October 8, 2024, from https://cwsglobal.org/about/history/.

Church World Service. (1925). *Church World Service Records, 1925–1969* [Dataset]. The Burke Library, Union Theological Seminary. https://library

.columbia.edu/content/dam/libraryweb/locations/burke/fa/wab/ldpd_4492691.pdf.

Clark Moschella, M. (2002). Food, faith, and formation: A case study on the use of ethnography in pastoral theology and care. *Journal of Pastoral Theology, 12*(1), 75–87. https://doi.org/10.1179/jpt.2002.12.1.007.

Cleves, R. H. (2022). Real men don't eat quiche: Queer food and gendered nationalism in the late twentieth-century USA. *Gender & History, 34*(3), 614–631. https://doi.org/10.1111/1468-0424.12645.

Cohen, A. B., & Koenig, H. G. (2003). Religion, religiosity and spirituality in the biopsychosocial model of health and ageing. *Ageing International, 28*, 215–241. https://doi.org/10.1007/s12126-002-1005-1.

Cohen, A. B. (2009). Many forms of culture. *American Psychologist, 64*(3), 194–204. https://doi.org/10.1037/a0015308.

Cohen, A. B. (2015). Religion's profound influences on psychology: Morality, intergroup relations, self-construal, and enculturation. *Current Directions in Psychological Science, 24*(1), 77–82. https://doi.org/10.1177/0963721414553265.

Cohen, A. B. (2021). You can learn a lot about religion from food. *Current Opinion in Psychology, 40*, 1–5. https://doi.org/10.1016/j.copsyc.2020.07.032.

Cohen, J. F. W., Gorski, M. T., Gruber, S. A., Kurdziel, L. B. F., & Rimm, E. B. (2016). The effect of healthy dietary consumption on executive cognitive functioning in children and adolescents: A systematic review. *British Journal of Nutrition, 116*(6), 989–1000. https://doi.org/10.1017/S0007114516002877.

Colby, S., McDonald, L., & Adkison, G. (2012). Traditional Native American foods: Stories from Northern Plains elders. *Journal of Ecological Anthropology, 15*(1), 65–73. https://doi.org/10.5038/2162-4593.15.1.5.

Colding, J., & Folke, C. (1997). The relations among threatened species, their protection, and taboos. *Conservation Ecology, 1*(1). https://doi.org/10.5751/ES-00018-010106.

Congregation for the Doctrine of the Faith. (2003, July 24). *Circular Letter to all Presidents of the Episcopal Conferences concerning the use of low-gluten altar breads and mustum as matter for the celebration of the Eucharist*. www.vatican.va/roman_curia/congregations/cfaith/documents/rc_con_cfaith_doc_20030724_pane-senza-glutine_en.html.

Crane, J. K. (2017). *Eating Ethically: Religion and Science for a Better Diet*. Columbia University Press.

Dalen, J., Smith, B. W., Shelley, B. M. et al. (2010). Pilot study: Mindful Eating and Living (MEAL): Weight, eating behavior, and psychological outcomes associated with a mindfulness-based intervention for people with obesity.

Complementary Therapies in Medicine, *18*(6), 260–264. https://doi.org/10.1016/j.ctim.2010.09.008.

Datler, G., Jagodzinski, W., & Schmidt, P. (2013). Two theories on the test bench: Internal and external validity of the theories of Ronald Inglehart and Shalom Schwartz. *Social Science Research*, *42*(3), 906–925. https://doi.org/10.1016/j.ssresearch.2012.12.009.

De Wit, J. B., Stok, F. M., Smolenski, D. J. et al. (2015). Food culture in the home environment: Family meal practices and values can support healthy eating and self-regulation in young people in four European countries. *Applied Psychology: Health and Well-Being*, *7*(1), 22–40. https://doi.org/10.1111/aphw.12034.

Demmrich, S., Koppold-Liebscher, D., Klatte, C., Steckhan, N., & Ring, R. M. (2021). Effects of religious intermittent dry fasting on religious experience and mindfulness: A longitudinal study among Baha'is. *Psychology of Religion and Spirituality*, 15(4), 459–470. https://doi.org/10.1037/rel0000423.

Donkin, R. A. (2013). *Manna: An Historical Geography*. Springer.

Douglas, M. (1978). *Purity and Danger: An Analysis of Concepts of Pollution and Taboo*. Routledge & Kegan Paul.

Douglas, M. (2003). *Purity and Danger: An Analysis of Concepts of Pollution and Taboo*. Routledge.

Duggan, A. J. (2011). Conciliar law 1123–1215: The legislation of the four Lateran councils. In W. Hartmann & K. Pennington (Eds.), *The History of Medieval Canon Law in the Classical Period, 1140–1234: From Gratian to the decretals of Pope Gregory IX*. Catholic University of America Press, 318–366. https://doi.org/10.2307/j.ctt2853s5.

Dumont, L. (1980). *Homo Hierarchicus: The Caste System and Its Implications*. University of Chicago Press. https://books.google.com/books?hl=en&lr=&id=XsOtRGdvIigC&oi=fnd&pg=PR5&dq=Homo+hierarchicus&ots=g36bEFm01I&sig=zbL-_3lP1kIVKjTUDI9vM5Bz0hQ

Dunbar, R. I. M. (2017). Breaking bread: The functions of social eating. *Adaptive Human Behavior and Physiology*, *3*(3), 198–211. https://doi.org/10.1007/s40750-017-0061-4.

Durkheim, E. (1915). *The Elementary Forms of the Religious Life: A Study in Religious Sociology*. Macmillan.

Ekmekcioglu, C. (2020). Nutrition and longevity – From mechanisms to uncertainties. *Critical Reviews in Food Science and Nutrition*, 60(18), 3063–3082. www.tandfonline.com/doi/full/10.1080/10408398.2019.1676698.

Emmons, R. A., & Kneezel, T. T. (2005). Giving thanks: Spiritual and religious correlates of gratitude. *Journal of Psychology & Christianity*, *24*(2), 140–148.

Employment Div., Dept. of Human Resources of Ore. v. Smith, 494 US 872 (Supreme Court 1989).

Esposito, J. L. (2002). *What Everyone Needs to Know about Islam*. Oxford University Press.

Evans, B. (2014). Engaged Jain traditions and social non-violence: Ethnographic case studies of lay animal activists and service-oriented nuns. *CrossCurrents*, *64*(2), 202–218. https://doi.org/10.1353/cro.2014.a783380.

Feirstein, B. (1982). *Real Men Don't Each Quiche*. Pocket Books.

Fernandez, J. W. (1978). African religious movements. *Annual Review of Anthropology*, *7*, 195–234. https://doi.org/10.1146/annurev.an.07.100178.001211.

Fessler, D. M. T., & Navarrete, C. D. (2003). Meat is good to taboo: Dietary proscriptions as a product of the interaction of psychological mechanisms and social processes. *Journal of Cognition and Culture*, *3*(1), 1–40. https://doi.org/10.1163/156853703321598563.

Fitch, H. S., & Henderson, R. W. (2003). A backward glance at iguana exploitation. *Iguana*, *10*(3), 63–66.

Fond, G., Macgregor, A., Leboyer, M., & Michalsen, A. (2013). Fasting in mood disorders: Neurobiology and effectiveness. A review of the literature. *Psychiatry Research*, *209*(3), 253–258. https://doi.org/10.1016/j.psychres.2012.12.018.

Fontana, L., & Partridge, L. (2015). Promoting health and longevity through diet: From model organisms to humans. *Cell*, *161*(1), 106–118. https://doi.org/10.1016/j.cell.2015.02.020.

Fraser, G. E., & Shavlik, D. J. (2001). Ten years of life: Is it a matter of choice? *Archives of Internal Medicine*, *161*(13), 1645–1652. https://doi.org/10.1001/archinte.161.13.1645.

Frazer, J. G. (1951). *The Golden Bough*. Macmillan Press.

Fredrickson, B. L., Boulton, A. J., Firestine, A. M. et al. (2017). Positive emotion correlates of meditation practice: A comparison of mindfulness meditation and loving-kindness meditation. *Mindfulness*, *8*(6), 1623–1633. https://doi.org/10.1007/s12671-017-0735-9.

Golden, C., & Comaroff, J. (2015). The human health and conservation relevance of food taboos in northeastern Madagascar. *Ecology and Society*, *20*(2). https://doi.org/10.5751/ES-07590-200242

Gómez-Pinilla, F. (2008). Brain foods: The effects of nutrients on brain function. *Nature Reviews Neuroscience*, *9*(7), 568–578. https://doi.org/10.1038/nrn2421.

Gould, S. E. (1970). *Trichinosis in man and animals*. Springfield, Illinois: Charles C. Thomas.

Grapard, A. G. (2021). Japanese food offerings. *Japanese Journal of Religious Studies*, *48*(1), 165–185. https://doi.org/10.18874/jjrs.48.1.2021.

Grunert, S. C., & Juhl, H. J. (1995). Values, environmental attitudes, and buying of organic foods. *Journal of Economic Psychology*, *16*(1), 39–62. https://doi.org/10.1016/0167-4870(94)00034-8.

Hale, J. R., de Boer, J. Z., Chanton, J. P., & Spiller, H. A. (2003). Questioning the Delphic oracle. *Scientific American*, *289*(2), 66–73. https://doi.org/10.1038/scientificamerican0803-66.

Hall, D. L., Cohen, A. B., Meyer, K. K., Varley, A. H., & Brewer, G. A. (2015). Costly signaling increases trust, even across religious affiliations. *Psychological Science*, *26*(9), 1368–1376. https://doi.org/10.1177/0956797615576473.

Hanh, T. N., & Cheung, L. (2011). *Savor: Mindful Eating, Mindful Life* (Illustrated edition). HarperOne.

Harris, M. (2012). The abominable pig. In C. Counihan, P. Van Esterik, & C. M. Counihan (Eds.), *Food and Culture: A Reader*. Routledge, 73–85. http://ebookcentral.proquest.com/lib/asulib-ebooks/detail.action?docID=1097808.

Haupt, P. (1922). Manna, nectar, and ambrosia. *Proceedings of the American Philosophical Society*, *61*(3), 227–236.

Henrich, J., & Henrich, N. (2010). The evolution of cultural adaptations: Fijian food taboos protect against dangerous marine toxins. *Proceedings of the Royal Society B: Biological Sciences*, *277*(1701), 3715–3724. https://doi.org/10.1098/rspb.2010.1191.

Hobson, N. M., Schroeder, J., Risen, J. L., Xygalatas, D., & Inzlicht, M. (2018). The psychology of rituals: An integrative review and process-based framework. *Personality and Social Psychology Review*, *22*(3), 260–284. https://doi.org/10.31234/osf.io/98v3f.

Hofstede, G. (2001). *Culture's Consequences: Comparing Values, Behaviors, Institutions and Organizations across Nations*. SAGE.

Hofstede, G. (2011). Dimensionalizing cultures: The Hofstede model in context. *Online Readings in Psychology and Culture*, *2*(1). https://doi.org/10.9707/2307-0919.1014.

Holt, C. L., Roth, D. L., Huang, J., & Clark, E. M. (2018). Role of religious social support in longitudinal relationships between religiosity and health-related outcomes in African Americans. *Journal of Behavioral Medicine*, *41*(1), 62–73. https://doi.org/10.1007/s10865-017-9877-4.

Hutcherson, C., Seppala, E., & Gross, J. (2008). Loving-kindness meditation increases social connectedness. *Emotion*, *8*, 720–724. https://doi.org/10.1037/a0013237.

Imtiaz, A. (2022, July 27). The purest food on Earth? *BBC*. www.bbc.com/travel/article/20220726-the-purest-food-on-earth.

Inglehart, R., & Baker, W. E. (2000). Modernization, cultural change, and the persistence of traditional values. *American Sociological Review*, *65*(1), 19–51. https://doi.org/10.2307/2657288.

James, W. (1889). The psychology of belief. *Mind*, *14*(55), 321–352. https://doi.org/10.1093/mind/xiv.55.321.

James, W. (1902). *The Varieties of Religious Experience*. Harvard University Press.

Jeremias, J. (1949). The last supper. *The Journal of Theological Studies*, *50* (197/198), 1–10. https://doi.org/10.1093/jts/os-l.1.1.

Johnson, K. A., Cohen, A. B., & Okun, M. A. (2016). God is watching you ... But also watching over you: The influence of benevolent God representations on secular volunteerism among Christians. *Psychology of Religion and Spirituality*, *8*(4), 363–374. https://doi.org/10.1037/rel0000040.

Johnson, K. A., Li, Y. J., & Cohen, A. B. (2015). Fundamental social motives and the varieties of religious experience. *Religion, Brain & Behavior*, *5*(3), 197–231. https://doi.org/10.1080/2153599X.2014.918684.

Jost, J. T., Glaser, J., Kruglanski, A. W., & Sulloway, F. J. (2003). Political conservatism as motivated social cognition. *Psychological Bulletin*, *129*(3), 339–375. https://doi.org/10.1037/0033-2909.129.3.339.

Kasser, T., & Ryan, R. M. (1996). Further examining the American dream: Differential correlates of intrinsic and extrinsic goals. *Personality and Social Psychology Bulletin*, *22*(3), 280–287. https://doi.org/10.1177/0146167296223006.

Kay, A. C., Whitson, J. A., Gaucher, D., & Galinsky, A. D. (2009). Compensatory control: Achieving order through the mind, our institutions, and the heavens. *Current Directions in Psychological Science*, *18*(5), 264–268. https://doi.org/10.1111/j.1467-8721.2009.01649.x.

Kehoe, A. B. (2002). Thunder's pipe: The Blackfoot ritual year. *Cosmos*, *18*, 19–33.

Kieschnick, J. (2005). Buddhist vegetarianism in China. In R. Sterckx (Ed.), *Of Tripod and Palate: Food, Politics, and Religion in Traditional China* (pp. 186–212). Palgrave Macmillan. https://doi.org/10.1057/9781403979278_10.

Koenig, H. G., Hays, J. C., George, L. K. et al. (1997). Modeling the cross-sectional relationships between religion, physical health, social support, and depressive symptoms. *The American Journal of Geriatric Psychiatry*, *5*(2), 131–144. https://doi.org/10.1097/00019442-199700520-00006.

Koole, S. L., Meijer, M., & Remmers, C. (2017). Religious rituals as tools for adaptive self-regulation. *Religion, Brain & Behavior*, *7*(3), 250–253. https://doi.org/10.1080/2153599X.2016.1156562.

LaPier, R. R. (2018, June 15). How Native American food is tied to important sacred stories. *The Conversation.* http://theconversation.com/how-native-american-food-is-tied-to-important-sacred-stories-97770.

LaPier, R. R. (2020, February 10). How a Native American coming-of-age ritual is making a comeback. *The Conversation.* http://theconversation.com/how-a-native-american-coming-of-age-ritual-is-making-a-comeback-130524.

Lashley, C., & Lashley, C. (2016). Religious perspectives on hospitality. In Conrad Lashley (Ed.), *Routledge Handbook of Hospitality Studies* (pp. 111–120). Taylor & Francis.

Leiper, J. B., Molla, A. M., & Molla, A. M. (2003). Effects on health of fluid restriction during fasting in Ramadan. *European Journal of Clinical Nutrition, 57*, S30–S38. https://doi.org/10.1038/sj.ejcn.1601899.

Macy, G. (1994). The dogma of transubstantiation in the Middle Ages. *The Journal of Ecclesiastical History, 45*(1), 11–41. https://doi.org/10.1017/S0022046900016419.

Mahias, M. (1987). Milk and its transmutations in Indian society. *Food and Foodways, 2*(1), 265–288. https://doi.org/10.1080/07409710.1987.9961921.

Marshall, D. A. (2010). Temptation, tradition, and taboo: A theory of sacralization. *Sociological Theory, 28*(1), 64–90. https://doi.org/10.1111/j.1467-9558.2009.01366.x.

Maslow, A. H. (1943). A theory of human motivation. *Psychological Review, 50*(4), 370–396. https://doi.org/10.1037/h0054346.

McCullough, M. E., Emmons, R. A., & Tsang, J.-A. (2002). The grateful disposition: A conceptual and empirical topography. *Journal of Personality and Social Psychology, 82*(1), 112–127. https://doi.org/10.1037//0022-3514.82.1.112.

McCullough, M. E., Enders, C. K., Brion, S. L., & Jain, A. R. (2005). The varieties of religious development in adulthood: A longitudinal investigation of religion and rational choice. *Journal of Personality and Social Psychology, 89*(1), 78–89. https://doi.org/10.1037/0022-3514.89.1.78.

McCullough, M. E., Friedman, H. S., Enders, C. K. et al. (2009). Does devoutness delay death? Psychological investment in religion and its association with longevity in the Terman sample. *Journal of Personality and Social Psychology, 97*(5), 866–882. https://doi.org/10.1037/a0016366.

McCullough, M. E., Hoyt, W. T., Larson, D. B., Koenig, H. G., & Thoresen, C. (2000). Religious involvement and mortality: A meta-analytic review. *Health Psychology, 19*(3), 211–222. http://dx.doi.org.ezproxy1.lib.asu.edu/10.1037/0278-6133.19.3.211.

McCullough, M. E., & Willoughby, B. (2009). Religion, self-regulation, and self-control: Associations, explanations, and implications. *Psychological Bulletin, 135*, 69–93. https://doi.org/10.1037/a0014213.

Mehran, J. (2019). The meaning of hospitality in Iran. In *Experiencing Persian Heritage* (Vol. 10, pp. 155–167). Emerald. https://doi.org/10.1108/S2042-144320190000010010.

Meigs, A. S. (1978). A Papuan perspective on pollution. *Man, 13*(2), 304–318. https://doi.org/10.2307/2800251.

Merrill, R. M. (2004). Life expectancy among LDS and non-LDS in Utah. *Demographic Research, 10,* 61–82. https://doi.org/10.4054/demres.2004.10.3.

Meyer-Rochow, V. B. (2009). Food taboos: Their origins and purposes. *Journal of Ethnobiology and Ethnomedicine, 5*(1), 18. https://doi.org/10.1186/1746-4269-5-18.

Meyer, B. (2004). Christianity in Africa: From African independent to Pentecostal-charismatic churches. *Annual Review of Anthropology, 33,* 447–474. https://doi.org/10.1146/annurev.anthro.33.070203.143835.

Meyer-Rochow, V. B. (2009). Food taboos: Their origins and purposes. *Journal of Ethnobiology and Ethnomedicine, 5*(1), 18. https://doi.org/10.1186/1746-4269-5-18.

Michalsen, A. (2010). Prolonged fasting as a method of mood enhancement in chronic pain syndromes: A review of clinical evidence and mechanisms. *Current Pain and Headache Reports, 14*(2), 80–87. https://doi.org/10.1007/s11916-010-0104-z.

Miller, H. V., Barnes, J. C., & Beaver, K. M. (2011). Self-control and health outcomes in a nationally representative sample. *American Journal of Health Behavior, 35*(1), 15–27. https://doi.org/10.5993/AJHB.35.1.2.

Mofokeng, T. R. (2024). Reconsidering syncretism and contextualization: The sangoma-prophet phenomenon in South African neo-prophetic Pentecostalism. *Religions, 15*(1), Article 84. https://doi.org/10.3390/rel15010084.

Moon, J. W., Cohen, A. B., Laurin, K., & MacKinnon, D. P. (2023). Is religion special? *Perspectives on Psychological Science, 18*(2), 340–357. https://doi.org/10.1177/17456916221100485.

Nash, H. S. (1913). The nature and definition of religion. *The Harvard Theological Review, 6*(1), 1–30. https://doi.org/10.1017/s001781600002945x.

Nemeroff, C., & Rozin, P. (1989). "You are what you eat": Applying the demand-free "impressions" technique to an unacknowledged belief. *Ethos, 17*(1), 50–69. https://doi.org/10.1525/eth.1989.17.1.02a00030.

Norman, C. E. (2012). Food and religion. In Jeffrey M. Pilcher (Ed.). *The Oxford Handbook of Food History, 1,* 409–426.

Northover, S. B., Quillien, T., Conroy-Beam, D., & Cohen, A. B. (2024). Religious signaling and prosociality: A review of the literature. *Evolution and Human Behavior, 45*(5), 106593. https://doi.org/10.1016/j.evolhumbehav.2024.06.002.

O'Connor, K. (2008). The Hawaiian Luau: Food as tradition, transgression, transformation, and travel. *Food, Culture & Society, 11*(2), 149–172. https://doi.org/10.2752/175174408X317543.

Olson, R., Knepple Carney, A., & Hicks Patrick, J. (2019). Associations between gratitude and spirituality: An experience sampling approach. *Psychology of Religion and Spirituality, 11*(4), 449–452. https://doi.org/10.1037/rel0000164.

Oman, D. (2013). Spiritual modeling and the social learning of spirituality and religion. In *APA handbook of psychology, religion, and spirituality (Vol 1): Context, theory, and research* (pp. 187–204). American Psychological Association. https://doi.org/10.1037/14045-010.

Orlich, M. J., Singh, P. N., Sabaté, J. et al. (2013). Vegetarian dietary patterns and mortality in Adventist Health Study 2. *JAMA Internal Medicine, 173*(13), 1230–1238. https://doi.org/10.1001/jamainternmed.2013.6473.

Panja, T. (2024, April 3). How Soccer learned to embrace Ramadan: From faked injuries to Bespoke Diets. *The New York Times*. www.nytimes.com/2024/04/03/world/europe/premier-league-ramadan.html?unlocked_article_code=1.WE4.RovN.1BqzHFZQ5nLr&smid=nytcore-ios-share&referringSource=articleShare.

Paquet, C., St-Arnaud-McKenzie, D., Ma, Z. et al. (2008). More than just not being alone: The number, nature, and complementarity of meal-time social interactions influence food intake in hospitalized elderly patients. *The Gerontologist, 48*(5), 603–611. https://doi.org/10.1093/geront/48.5.603.

Pargament, K. I., Smith, B. W., Koenig, H. G., & Perez, L. (1998). Patterns of positive and negative religious coping with major life stressors. *Journal for the Scientific Study of Religion*, 710–724. https://doi.org/10.2307/1388152.

Park, J., Bonn, M. A., & Cho, M. (2020). Sustainable and religion food consumer segmentation: Focusing on Korean temple food restaurants. *Sustainability, 12*(7), 3035. https://doi.org/10.3390/su12073035.

Pérez, E. (2011). Cooking for the gods: Sensuous ethnography, sensory knowledge, and the kitchen in Lucumí tradition. *Religion, 41*(4), 665–683. https://doi.org/10.1080/0048721x.2011.619585.

Pérez, E. (2014). Crystallizing subjectivities in the African diaspora: Sugar, honey, and the gods of Afro-Cuban Lucumí. In B. E. Zeller, M. W. Dallam, R. L. Neilson, & N. L. Rubel (Eds.), *Religion, Food, and Eating in North America* (pp. 175–194). Columbia University Press. www.degruyterbrill.com/document/doi/10.7312/zell16030-011/html.

Pérez, E. (2016). *Religion in the Kitchen: Cooking, Talking, and the Making of Black Atlantic Traditions*. New York University Press. https://doi.org/10.18574/nyu/9781479861613.001.0001.

Perry, G. H., Dominy, N. J., Claw, K. G. et al. (2007). Diet and the evolution of human amylase gene copy number variation. *Nature Genetics*, *39*(10), 1256–1260. https://doi.org/10.1038/ng2123.

Persynaki, A., Karras, S., & Pichard, C. (2017). Unraveling the metabolic health benefits of fasting related to religious beliefs: A narrative review. *Nutrition*, *35*, 14–20. https://doi.org/10.1016/j.nut.2016.10.005.

Peter, A., Ishulutak, M., Shaimaiyuk, J. et al. (2002). The seal: An integral part of our culture. *Études/Inuit/Studies*, *26*(1), 167–174. https://doi.org/10.7202/009276ar.

Pew Research Center. (2006, October 5). Overview: Pentecostalism in Africa. *Pew Research Center*. www.pewresearch.org/religion/2006/10/05/overview-pentecostalism-in-africa/.

Pew Research Center. (2012). *The Global Religious Landscape: A Report on the Size and Distribution of the World's Major Religious Groups as of 2010.* https://assets.pewresearch.org/wp-content/uploads/sites/11/2014/01/global-religion-full.pdf.

Pollan, M. (2010). *The omnivore's dilemma: The secrets behind what you eat.*

Powell, J. (2021). Ital hermeneutics: The innovative theological grounding of Rastafari dietary (ietary) practices. *Black Theology*, *19*(1), 32–52. https://doi.org/10.1080/14769948.2021.1897097.

Purnell, D., & Jenkins, J. (2013). Breaking bread, creating community: Food's ability to increase communal ties and relationships. *Florida Communication Journal*, *41*, 73–84.

Rad, M. S. (2023). From self-deprivation to cooperation: How Ramadan fasting influences risk-aversion and decisions in resource dilemmas. *Current Research in Ecological and Social Psychology*, *5*, 100152. https://doi.org/10.1016/j.cresp.2023.100152.

Rahman, S. A. (2017). Religion and animal welfare – An Islamic perspective. *Animals*, *7*(2), 11. https://doi.org/10.3390/ani7020011.

Randall, T. E. (2016). Meat and the crisis of masculinity. In Mary Rawlinson, Caleb Ward (Eds.). *The Routledge Handbook of Food Ethics*, Routledge: USA, 72–81.

Ring, R. M., Eisenmann, C., Kandil, F. I. et al. (2022). Mental and behavioural responses to Bahá'í fasting: Looking behind the scenes of a religiously motivated intermittent fast using a mixed methods approach. *Nutrients*, *14*(5), 1038. https://doi.org/10.3390/nu14051038.

Robinson, M. D., & Clore, G. L. (2002). Belief and feeling: Evidence for an accessibility model of emotional self-report. *Psychological Bulletin*, *128*(6), 934–960. https://doi.org/10.1037//0033-2909.128.6.934.

Roccas, S. (2005). Religion and value systems. *Journal of Social Issues*, *61*(4), 747–759. https://doi.org/10.1111/j.1540-4560.2005.00430.x.

Rohrer, J. R. (1990). The origins of the temperance movement: A reinterpretation. *Journal of American Studies*, *24*(2), 228–235. https://doi.org/10.1017/s0021875800029753.

Rosmarin, D. H., Pirutinsky, S., Cohen, A. B., Galler, Y., & Krumrei, E. J. (2011). Grateful to God or just plain grateful? A comparison of religious and general gratitude. *The Journal of Positive Psychology*, *6*(5), 389–396. https://doi.org/10.1080/17439760.2011.596557.

Rothgerber, H. (2013). Real men don't eat (vegetable) quiche: Masculinity and the justification of meat consumption. *Psychology of Men & Masculinities*, *14*(4), 363–375. https://doi.org/10.1037/a0030379.

Rounding, K., Lee, A., Jacobson, J. A., & Ji, L.-J. (2012). Religion replenishes self-control. *Psychological Science*, *23*(6), 635–642. https://doi.org/10.1177/0956797611431987.

Rozin, P. (1976). The Selection of Foods by Rats, Humans, and Other Animals. *Advances in the Study of Behavior*, 21–76. https://doi.org/10.1016/s0065-3454(08)60081-9.

Rozin, P. (2014). Social and moral aspects of food and eating. In Irvin Rock (Ed.). *The Legacy of Solomon Asch* (pp. 97–110). Psychology Press.

Rozin, P., Ashmore, M., & Markwith, M. (1996). Lay American conceptions of nutrition: Dose insensitivity, categorical thinking, contagion, and the monotonic mind. *Health Psychology*, *15*(6), 438–447. https://doi.org/10.1037//0278-6133.15.6.438.

Rozin, P., Hormes, J. M., Faith, M. S., & Wansink, B. (2012). Is meat male? A quantitative multimethod framework to establish metaphoric relationships. *Journal of Consumer Research*, *39*(3), 629–643. https://doi.org/10.1086/664970.

Rozin, P., Lowery, L., & Ebert, R. (1994). Varieties of disgust faces and the structure of disgust. *Journal of Personality and Social Psychology*, *66*(5), 870–881. https://doi.org/10.1037//0022-3514.66.5.870.

Rozin, P., Markwith, M., & Nemeroff, C. (1992). Magical contagion beliefs and fear of AIDS. *Journal of Applied Social Psychology*, *22*(14), 1081–1092. https://doi.org/10.1111/j.1559-1816.1992.tb00943.x.

Rozin, P., Ruby, M. B., & Cohen, A. B. (2019). Food and eating. In S. Kitayama & D. Cohen (Eds.), *Handbook of Cultural Psychology* (2nd ed., pp. 447–477). Guilford.

Rushing, J. R. (2008). Origins and celebrations of El Día de Los Muertos. *Death Lore: Texas Rituals, Superstitions, and Legends of the Hereafter*, *65*, 147–151.

Sagiv, L., & Schwartz, S. H. (2000). Value priorities and subjective well-being: Direct relations and congruity effects. *European Journal of Social Psychology, 30*(2), 177–198. https://doi.org/10.1002/(sici)1099-0992(200003/04)30:2%3C177::aid-ejsp982%3E3.0.co;2-z.

Sagiv, L., & Schwartz, S. H. (2022). Personal values across cultures. *Annual Review of Psychology, 73*, 517–546. https://doi.org/10.1146/annurev-psych-020821-125100.

Sangave, V. A. (1980). *Jaina Community: A Social Survey.* Popular Prakashan.

Sarlo, M., Buodo, G., Poli, S., & Palomba, D. (2005). Changes in EEG alpha power to different disgust elicitors: The specificity of mutilations. *Neuroscience Letters, 382*(3), 291–296. https://doi.org/10.1016/j.neulet.2005.03.037.

Saroglou, V. (2011). Believing, bonding, behaving, and belonging: The big four religious dimensions and cultural variation. *Journal of Cross-Cultural Psychology, 42*(8), 1320–1340. https://doi.org/10.1177/0022022111412267.

Saroglou, V., Clobert, M., Cohen, A. B. et al. (2020). Believing, bonding, behaving, and belonging: The cognitive, emotional, moral, and social dimensions of religiousness across cultures. *Journal of Cross-Cultural Psychology, 51*(7), 551–575. https://doi.org/10.1177/0022022120946488.

Saroglou, V., Delpierre, V., & Dernelle, R. (2004). Values and religiosity: A meta-analysis of studies using Schwartz's model. *Personality and Individual Differences, 37*(4), 721–734. https://doi.org/10.1016/j.paid.2003.10.005.

Schutt, W. A., Exline, J. J., Pait, K. C., & Wilt, J. A. (2024). Psychedelic experiences and long-term spiritual growth: A systematic review. *Current Psychology, 43*(32), 26372–26394. https://doi.org/10.1007/s12144-024-06272-2.

Schwartz, S. H. (1992). Universals in the content and structure of values: Theoretical advances and empirical tests in 20 countries. In Mark P. Zanna (Eds.). *Advances in Experimental Social Psychology* (Vol. 25, pp. 1–65). Elsevier. https://doi.org/10.1016/s0065-2601(08)60281-6.

Schwartz, S. H. (2007). Value orientations: Measurement, antecedents and consequences across nations. In R. Jowell, C. Roberts, R. Fitzgerald, & G. Eva (Eds.), *Measuring Attitudes Cross-Nationally* (pp. 169–203). SAGE, Ltd. https://doi.org/10.4135/9781849209458.n9.

Schwartz, S. H. (2012). An overview of the Schwartz theory of basic values. *Online Readings in Psychology and Culture, 2*(1). https://doi.org/10.9707/2307-0919.1116.

Sen, C. T. (2007). Jainism: The world's most ethical religion. In Susan R. Friedland (Ed.). *Food and Morality: Proceedings of the Oxford Symposium on Food and Cookery 2007*, pp. 230–240. https://books.google.com/books?hl=en&lr=&id=xYpRi5gLZHIC&oi=fnd&pg=PT230&dq=jainism+food&ots=od1vHSKayz&sig=c4sb1vnYtzFJbcCUahogSrj7Rx4.

Settles, I., & Buchanan, N. T. (2014). Multiple Groups, Multiple Identities, and Intersectionality. In V. Benet-Martínez & Y. Hong (Eds.), *The Oxford Handbook of Multicultural Identity* (pp. 160–180). Oxford University Press. https://doi.org/10.1093/oxfordhb/9780199796694.013.017.

Shams, L., & Seitz, A. R. (2008). Benefits of multisensory learning. *Trends in Cognitive Sciences, 12*(11), 411–417. https://doi.org/10.1016/j.tics.2008.07.006.

Shariff, A. F., & Rhemtulla, M. (2012). Divergent effects of beliefs in heaven and hell on national crime rates. *PLOS ONE, 7*(6), e39048. https://doi.org/10.1371/journal.pone.0039048.

Sharma, J. (2021). Symbolism of food in Hinduism. *Anthropology, 9*(8), 1–4. https://doi.org/10.35248/2332-0915.21.9.252.

Shatila, H., Baroudi, M., El Sayed Ahmad, R. et al. (2021). Impact of Ramadan fasting on dietary intakes among healthy adults: A year-round comparative study. *Frontiers in Nutrition, 8*. https://doi.org/10.3389/fnut.2021.689788.

Shaw, R., & Cassidy, T. (2022). Self-compassion, mindful eating, eating attitudes and wellbeing among emerging adults. *The Journal of Psychology, 156* (1), 33–47. https://doi.org/10.1080/00223980.2021.1992334.

Sherbert v. Verner, 374 US 398 (Supreme Court 526).

Sidanius, J., & Pratto, F. (2012). Social dominance theory. In P. A. M. Van Lange, A. W. Kruglanski, & E. T. Higgins (Eds.), *Handbook of theories of social psychology* (pp. 418–438). Sage Publications Ltd.

Signorelli, A. (2024, June 20). *The Health Benefits of Ghee*. www.vogue.com/article/health-benefits-of-ghee.

Singh, M., & Henrich, J. (2020). Why do religious leaders observe costly prohibitions? Examining taboos on Mentawai shamans. *Evolutionary Human Sciences, 2*, e32. https://doi.org/10.1017/ehs.2020.32.

Simoons, F. J. (1994). *Eat Not this Flesh: Food Avoidances from Prehistory to the Present*. University of Wisconsin Press.

Smith, B. K. (1990). Eaters, food, and social hierarchy in ancient India: A dietary guide to a revolution of values. *Journal of the American Academy of Religion, 58*(2), 177–205. https://doi.org/10.1093/jaarel/lviii.2.177.

Smith, G. A. (2019, August 5). Just one-third of U.S. Catholics agree with their church that Eucharist is body, blood of Christ. *Pew Research Center*. www.pewresearch.org/short-reads/2019/08/05/transubstantiation-eucharist-u-s-catholics/.

Sosis, R. (2003). Why aren't we all hutterites?: Costly signaling theory and religious behavior. *Human Nature, 14*(2), 91–127. https://doi.org/10.1007/s12110-003-1000-6.

Sosis, R. (2004). The adaptive value of religious ritual: Rituals promote group cohesion by requiring members to engage in behavior that is too costly to fake. *American Scientist, 92*(2), 166–172. https://www.jstor.org/stable/27858365.

Souza, P. (2015). Food in African Brazilian Candomblé. *Scripta Instituti Donneriani Aboensis, 26*, 264–280. https://doi.org/10.30674/scripta.67457.

Stapel, B., Fraccarollo, D., Westhoff-Bleck, M. et al. (2022). Impact of fasting on stress systems and depressive symptoms in patients with major depressive disorder: A cross-sectional study. *Scientific Reports, 12*(1), 7642. https://doi.org/10.1038/s41598-022-11639-1.

Stein, D. H., Hobson, N. M., & Schroeder, J. (2021). A sacred commitment: How rituals promote group survival. *Current Opinion in Psychology, 40*, 114–120. https://doi.org/10.1016/j.copsyc.2020.09.005.

Stockbridge, M. D., Bahouth, M. N., Zink, E. K., & Hillis, A. E. (2023). Socialize, eat more, and feel better: Communal eating in acute neurological care. *American Journal of Physical Medicine & Rehabilitation, 102*(2S), S38–S42. https://doi.org/10.1097/PHM.0000000000002123.

Streng, F. J. (1972). Studying Religion: Possibilities and limitations of different definitions. *Journal of the American Academy of Religion, 40*(2), 219–237. https://doi.org/10.1093/jaarel/xl.1.219.

Stross, B. (2010). This world and beyond: Food practices and the social order in Mayan religion. In J. Staller & M. Carrasco (Eds.), *Pre-Columbian Foodways: Interdisciplinary Approaches to Food, Culture, and Markets in Ancient Mesoamerica* (pp. 553–576). Springer. https://doi.org/10.1007/978-1-4419-0471-3_23.

Sullivan, A. R. (2010). Mortality differentials and religion in the U.S.: Religious affiliation and attendance. *Journal for the Scientific Study of Religion, 49*(4), 740–753. https://doi.org/10.1111/j.1468-5906.2010.01543.x.

Tamney, J. B. (1986). Fasting and dieting: A research note. *Review of Religious Research, 27*(3), 255–262. https://doi.org/10.2307/3511420.

Taylor, S. E. (2011). Social Support: A Review. In H. S. Friedman (Ed.), *The Oxford Handbook of Health Psychology* (pp. 190–214). Oxford University Press. https://doi.org/10.1093/oxfordhb/9780195342819.013.0009.

Terrizzi, J. A. (2017). Is religion an evolutionarily evoked disease-avoidance strategy? *Religion, Brain & Behavior, 7*(4), 328–330. https://doi.org/10.1080/2153599X.2016.1249918.

The Fourth Lateran Council. (1215). N. P. Tanner, Trans., Vol. 1. Georgetown University Press.

Tinbergen, N. (1963). On aims and methods of ethology. *Zeitschrift Für Tierpsychologie, 20*(4), 410–433. https://doi.org/10.1111/j.1439-0310.1963.tb01161.x.

Tinsley, G. M., & La Bounty, P. M. (2015). Effects of intermittent fasting on body composition and clinical health markers in humans. *Nutrition Reviews*, *73*(10), 661–674. https://doi.org/10.1093/nutrit/nuv041.

Tomlinson, M. (2007). Everything and its opposite: Kava drinking in Fiji. *Anthropological Quarterly*, *80*(4), 1065–1081. https://doi.org/10.1353/anq.2007.0054.

Tong, E. M. W., Tan, K. W. T., Chor, A. A. B. et al. (2016). Humility facilitates higher self-control. *Journal of Experimental Social Psychology*, *62*, 30–39. https://doi.org/10.1016/J.JESP.2015.09.008.

Trepanowski, J. F., & Bloomer, R. J. (2010). The impact of religious fasting on human health. *Nutrition Journal*, *9*(1), 57. https://doi.org/10.1186/1475-2891-9-57

Trombley, J. (n.d.). American Indian Health and Diet Project. Retrieved July 15, 2025, from https://aihd.ku.edu/foods/prairie_turnip.html.

Tsang, J.-A., Schulwitz, A., & Carlisle, R. D. (2012). An experimental test of the relationship between religion and gratitude. *Psychology of Religion and Spirituality*, *4*(1), 40–55. https://doi.org/10.1037/a0025632.

Tseng, A. A. (2018). Five influential factors for Chinese Buddhists' vegetarianism. *Worldviews: Global Religions, Culture, and Ecology*, *22*(2), 143–162. https://doi.org/10.1163/15685357-02201100.

Tybur, J. M., Lieberman, D., & Griskevicius, V. (2009). Microbes, mating, and morality: Individual differences in three functional domains of disgust. *Journal of Personality and Social Psychology*, *97*(1), 103–122. https://doi.org/10.1037/a0015474.

Uchiyama, R., Spicer, R., & Muthukrishna, M. (2021). Cultural evolution of genetic heritability. *Behavioral and Brain Sciences*, *45*, e152. https://doi.org/10.1017/S0140525X21000893.

Ugur, Z. B. (2021). Does self-control foster generosity? Evidence from ego depleted children. *Journal of Behavioral and Experimental Economics*, *90* (November 2020), 101652. https://doi.org/10.1016/j.socec.2020.101652.

Urkin, J., & Naimer, S. (2015). Jewish holidays and their associated medical risks. *Journal of Community Health*, *40*(1), 82–87. https://doi.org/10.1007/s10900-014-9899-6.

Vail, K. E., Arndt, J., & Abdollahi, A. (2012). Exploring the existential function of religion and supernatural agent beliefs among Christians, Muslims, atheists, and agnostics. *Personality and Social Psychology Bulletin*, *38*(10), 1288–1300. https://doi.org/10.1177/0146167212449361.

Vail, K. E., Rothschild, Z. K., Weise, D. et al. (2009). *A Terror Management Analysis of the Psychological Functions of Religion*. https://doi.org/10.1177/1088868309351165.

Van Cappellen, P., Saroglou, V., & Toth-Gauthier, M. (2016). Religiosity and prosocial behavior among churchgoers: Exploring underlying mechanisms. *The International Journal for the Psychology of Religion, 26*(1), 19–30. https://doi.org/10.1080/10508619.2014.958004.

Van Tongeren, D. R., DeWall, C. N., Chen, Z., Sibley, C. G., & Bulbulia, J. (2021). Religious residue: Cross-cultural evidence that religious psychology and behavior persist following deidentification. *Journal of Personality and Social Psychology, 120*(2), 484–503. https://doi.org/10.1037/pspp0000288.

Viskupič, F., & Wiltse, D. L. (2022). The messenger matters: Religious leaders and overcoming COVID-19 vaccine hesitancy. *PS: Political Science & Politics, 55*(3), 504–509. https://doi.org/10.1017/S104909652200004X.

Vogt, E. Z. (1976). *Tortillas for the Gods: A Symbolic Analysis of Zinacanteco Rituals*. Harvard University Press.

Wallace, L. E., Anthony, R., End, C. M., & Way, B. M. (2019). Does religion stave off the grave? Religious affiliation in one's obituary and longevity. *Social Psychological and Personality Science, 10*(5), 662–670. https://doi.org/10.1177/1948550618779820.

Wansink, B., & Sobal, J. (2007). Mindless eating: The 200 daily food decisions we overlook. *Environment and Behavior, 39*(1), 106–123. https://doi.org/10.1177/0013916506295573.

Warren, J. M., Smith, N., & Ashwell, M. (2017). A structured literature review on the role of mindfulness, mindful eating and intuitive eating in changing eating behaviours: Effectiveness and associated potential mechanisms. *Nutrition Research Reviews, 30*(2), 272–283. https://doi.org/10.1017/S0954422417000154.

Whitehead, B. (2018). Religiousness on mental health in older adults: The mediating role of social support and healthy behaviours. *Mental Health, Religion & Culture, 21*(4), 429–441. https://doi.org/10.1080/13674676.2018.1504906.

World Health Organization. (2009). Religious and cultural aspects of hand hygiene. In *WHO Guidelines on Hand Hygiene in Health Care: First Global Patient Safety Challenge Clean Care Is Safer Care*. www.ncbi.nlm.nih.gov/books/NBK143998/.

Wormald, B. (2015, April 2). The future of world religions: Population growth projections, 2010–2050. *Pew Research Center*. https://pewresearch.org/religion/2015/04/02/religious-projections-2010-2050/.

Wormley, A. S., & Cohen, A. B. (2022). Pathogen prevalence and food taboos: A cross-cultural analysis. *Current Research in Ecological and Social Psychology, 3*, 100056. https://doi.org/10.1016/j.cresp.2022.100056.

References

Wormley, A. S., Moon, J. W., Johnson, K. A. et al. (accepted in principle). Morality of mentality and culture: A registered replication and cross-cultural extension. *International Journal for the Psychology of Religion*.

Wormley, A. S., Vornlocher, C., Aglozo, E. Y., Jayawickreme, E., Johnson, K. A., Moon, J. W., Van Cappellen, P., Verma, A., & Cohen, A. B. (2025). Religion and human flourishing. *The Journal of Positive Psychology, 20*(1), 43–58. https://doi.org/10.1080/17439760.2023.2297208.

Wu, E. S. (2018). Chinese Ancestral Worship. In C. K. Cann (Ed.), *Dying to Eat: Cross-Cultural Perspectives on Food, Death, and the Afterlife* (pp. 17–36). University Press of Kentucky.

Xiong, W. (2023). Food culture, religious belief and community relations: An ethnographic study of the overseas Chinese Catholic. *Religions, 14*(2), Article 2. https://doi.org/10.3390/rel14020207.

Zanni, D. G. (2008). Ambrosia, nectar and elaion in the Homeric poems. In S. A. Paipetis (Ed.), *Science and Technology in Homeric Epics* (pp. 391–399). Springer. https://doi.org/10.1007/978-1-4020-8784-4_31.

Cambridge Elements =

Psychology of Religion

Jonathan Lewis-Jong
St Mary's University Twickenham and University of Oxford

Jonathan Lewis-Jong is Researcher in Psychology of Religion at the Benedict XVI Centre for Religion and Society at St Mary's University, Twickenham, and an Associate of the Ian Ramsey Centre for Science and Religion at the University of Oxford. His recent books include *Experimenting with Religion* (2023) and *Death Anxiety and Religion Belief* (2016). He is also an Associate Editor at the American Psychological Association journal *Psychology of Religion and Spirituality*.

Editorial Board
Paul Bloom, *University of Toronto*
Adam B. Cohen, *Arizona State University*
Ara Norenzayan, *University of British Columbia*
Crystal Park, *University of Connecticut*
Aiyana Willard, *Brunel University*
Jacqueline Woolley, *University of Texas at Austin*

About the Series
This series offers authoritative introductions to central topics in the psychology of religion, covering the psychological causes, consequences, and correlates of religion, as well as conceptual and methodological issues. The Elements reflect diverse perspectives, including from developmental, evolutionary, cognitive, social, personality and clinical psychology, and neuroscience.

Cambridge Elements

Psychology of Religion

Elements in the Series

Divination: A Cognitive Perspective
Ze Hong

Morality and the Gods
Benjamin Grant Purzycki

Religion and Food
Alexandra S. Wormley and Adam B. Cohen

A full series listing is available at: www.cambridge.org/EPOR

For EU product safety concerns, contact us at Calle de José Abascal, 56–1°,
28003 Madrid, Spain or eugpsr@cambridge.org.

www.ingramcontent.com/pod-product-compliance
Lightning Source LLC
LaVergne TN
LVHW020006080526
838200LV00081B/4399